HOCKEY:
The Sports Playbook

Red Kelly with Martin Lader

HOCKEY:
The Sports Playbook

illustrated by Tony Pannoni

Doubleday & Company, Inc.
Garden City, New York   1976

Photo credits: pp. xii, 4, 16, 22, 56, 68, 82, 90, 98 Courtesy Spectra-Action; 8, 12, 34, 44, 52, 66, 74 Courtesy Wide-World; 42 Courtesy Leonard Keran.

Library of Congress Cataloging in Publication Data

Kelly, Red.
Hockey: the sports playbook.

1. Hockey coaching. I. Lader, Martin, joint author. II. Title.
GV848.25.K44   796.9′62
ISBN: 0-385-06045-9
Library of Congress Catalog Card Number 75–40731

PREFACE

Hockey has been a part of my life since that long-ago day when I first laced on my older brother's skates and took a stumbling turn around the frozen-over cedar swamps in our hometown of Simcoe, Ontario. I was barely four years old at the time, and I had to put on several pairs of socks just so the skates would stay on.

Through the rest of my childhood, my teens, my early manhood, and now even in my middle years, I have played the game of hockey and made it my business. And in my fifth decade in the game, I still consider it one of the greatest sports in the world.

This is a game, I discovered, that prepares you for life, a wonderful introduction that will leave you better able to cope with various situations and personalities. Hockey is by no means a soft sport, a game that you can wander into lackadaisically as you would a game of catch. It demands conditioning and concentration and planning, and if you are willing to pay hockey its due, it will return its own rewards even if you have no desire to attain a professional level.

Although each individual is essential to the overall effort, and indeed everyone on the ice is his own quarterback, hockey is above all a team game. No matter how great the individual star, everyone must be prepared to help each other out. A selfish team is not a winning team.

This is one of the basics a smart youngster learns when he joins his first team, as well as the ability to get along with people. There are all kinds of individuals playing the game, some with tempers and some without, some who are introverts and others who are extroverts, some who will utilize every opportunity to bend the rules, some who are overly aggressive and others who are too timid, and so on. Any person who can take from hockey only these two fundamentals—the ability to work with others and to get along with them—is one up on life when he enters the business world.

In addition to the effect of building character and the mind, hockey also has the physical effect of building the body and stamina. You can always tell a skater when you see one by the muscles on his legs and calves.

As a youngster, my dream always was to play in the National Hockey League and, unlike many other people who reach a certain goal, I have never really been disappointed. And even if I hadn't been good enough to reach the top, I still wouldn't have regretted the many years I devoted to the game while growing up.

Hockey is a very precise game, one that requires refined skills as well as pure muscle. It is not an easy trick, for example, to pass the puck to a teammate who is skating away from you at a speed of thirty miles per hour, nor is it easy to concentrate your efforts on finding a small chink in the goaltender's armor when a snarling defenseman is about to knock you off your feet.

In this book, I will try to share with you some of the technical knowledge I have acquired in my more than forty years on skates. But the only way these words can be usefully utilized is if you are willing to complement them with adequate skating time of your own. During the rest of this Preface I would like to dwell on what might be termed the ethics of hockey, as well as other related topics.

Let's start with the simple truth that no one likes to be knocked on his behind, whether he's playing on a desolate ice pond or before eighteen thousand people in a National Hockey League arena. But this is an essential part of the game, and there is no one who can avoid an occasional dumping. There is no need to feel humiliation at taking a check and being knocked down, and it will never help your cause one bit to lose your head over it.

If you get bowled over, get back on your feet as quick as you can and skate back into the play. This doesn't mean you should smile over it. Nor does it mean you should be seeking vengeance. It does mean that you've been taken out of the play, and until you can catch up with it again your team will be at a disadvantage.

You must learn to keep control of yourself during the heat of battle. You do neither yourself, nor your team, a service if you do something rash and take a stupid penalty. Many a game and many a championship have been lost by a team while one player on that team was sitting unnecessarily in the penalty box.

At the same time, you can never allow yourself to be intimidated by another player. There will always be players on other teams who will test you and see how far you will bend. If they find that you are thrown off by body contact, they will be after you every turn on ice.

You must be prepared to hit rival skaters if you are to become an accomplished player. Forceful checking and body contact are integral parts of the game, and it is important to learn how to hit people with your body—but legally, without breaking the rules and without attempting to cause injury.

There are those people who cannot play within the rules because they don't have the ability to do so. This is certainly a drawback and will curtail their careers in hockey.

How aggressive should you be? No one should go out with the intent to inflict serious injury. But you still must be tough enough that when you give someone a hip check he'll feel it for a while. If a person is well-conditioned, he can take a solid bodycheck without much risk of injury.

Whatever the heat of action and the temperament of feelings, remember that the stick you carry in your hands can be a lethal weapon if used in the wrong way. The stick is to be used only to handle and carry the puck, and sometimes as a protective buffer if you're going into the boards or if a rival player is about to throw a check at you.

In all but a sprinkling of cases, grudges do not last very long in hockey. Just as you find in going to school, or in business, there are certain person- alities who are likely to clash and seemingly can't coexist together. And, not so surprisingly, sometimes after further contact you find the other person isn't quite as bad as you thought at first.

Because of the rapid pace at which the game is played, and the integral body contact, conditioning is essential for a hockey player. If you are in ex- cellent condition, you will derive the full potential of whatever ability you possess. But if you are only 50 per cent fit, you will be able to put out only 50 per cent of your potential. In addition to physical development, proper condi- tioning also includes a healthy diet and enough rest.

In hockey, players are called upon to operate in quick bursts, just as a sprinter does. Between these bursts, there are occasional coasting periods, when not much is happening. Then suddenly you're going again, chasing someone down ice, backchecking, then quickly turning around and racing to- ward the other end of the ice. To do this, you must have good wind and good recuperative powers, and of course while you are doing this you must expect to get hit from time to time.

Picture a sprinter who's racing away for dear life and suddenly gets hit by a runner going the other way. That's an awful jolt, and I doubt that too many sprinters would be able to get back on their feet and continue running. In hockey, the unexpected jolt must always be expected, and from any direction.

A player who is prepared, and who is conditioned, can at least avoid being hit head-on. The key to accomplishing this is to be in full control of your feet and your body so that when you are getting hit, you have the balance to spin and roll away from the major impact of the blow. If you cannot control your- self, you will be dealt a smashing blow.

The best way to minimize the possibility of injury is to be in the best shape possible. Hockey players are notorious for their ability to bounce back from injury, and it is a fact that doctors have learned things about medicine as a re- sult of their contact with athletes.

One example is the common charley horse. We knew as kids that if you got hit in the big muscle in your thigh and it started to hurt, the best thing to do was to keep going. If you sat down immediately and left the leg motionless, you would find the muscle harden like a rock and become so sore you proba- bly wouldn't be able to go out and play any more.

But if you kept on skating, the blow would have caused some internal bleeding but the movement of the muscle took that blood and dispersed it, eliminating the hardening effect.

It would be silly to deny that there is no danger of being hurt, even for a youngster, while playing the game of hockey. But to borrow a worn cliché, you can get hurt crossing the street. There is a danger in anything you do. But if you're trained, and in good condition, and have an idea of what the game is about, and don't play above your level, there is relatively little chance of suffering a serious injury. Bumps and bruises we're all going to get.

This, then, is the game of hockey, a miniature version of life itself. You'll get hurt and often, but you'll learn to get yourself up, react to situations, and fight back.

CONTENTS

Preface   v

Skating   1

Passing   5

Shooting   9

Maneuverability   13

Faceoffs   17

Offense with Both Sides Even   23

The Power Play   35

Defensing the Power Play   45

Defense with Both Sides Even   53

Breakaways   57

Defensing the Breakaway   69

Defensemen   75

Goaltenders   83

Checking   91

Rules Introduction   101

Official NHL Rules   103

HOCKEY:
The Sports Playbook

SKATING

It is elemental that to play hockey, on any level, you must be able to skate. How well you can skate, and how much you are able to improve, will help determine to a large degree how successful you will be in the game and how high you can climb.

Skating is one of the great equalizers in hockey, one of the reasons why a smaller person can enjoy just as great a success as a powerful, big man. Michel Briere, who played for me at Pittsburgh, was one of the smallest men in the league, but when he had his skates on there was no one who could touch him. He was like a wisp as he floated around the ice.

Davey Keon, who had a tremendous career with Toronto, is another good example. He weighed in at only about 165 pounds, yet he could check the biggest guys around and he gave those rugged defensemen a rough time when he went forechecking into their end. Keon was effective because he could start and stop on a dime, and probably could start quicker from a standing position than anyone.

Henri Richard, Ted Lindsay, and Stan Mikita are other examples of smaller-than-average players who were All-Star performers. These people were quick and mobile, and could maneuver on skates. They were able to anticipate what was coming and to bust for holes.

Camille Henry was as small as they come in hockey, and he couldn't stand in front of a net like a Jean Beliveau could and block the view of a goaltender while fighting off defensemen. Henry would move in front, and when someone gave him a shove he'd disappear, go around behind the net, and when the defenseman took his eyes off him, Henry would scoot out in front again. He could "feel" the puck very well, and take it out of the air as well as anyone I ever saw. He would have been a good bunter in baseball, because when the puck came flying through the air he could tick it and change its direction.

Yvan Cournoyer is stronger than Henry, but he's also small and quick as all get-out. He darts around and gets his shot away like a bullet. Just about everything he does is in double-time, and he's got a good wrist shot to boot.

The point of these examples is to show that there is definitely a place in

hockey for a small person, providing he doesn't allow other players to intimidate him. What he lacks in strength he can make up with speed and finesse.

The only way to be a good skater is by constant practicing. Learn to use your inside edges and your outside edges, learn to have the right balance and the right stride.

From a standing start, use short strides to get yourself started, then go into the longer stride for power once you've built momentum. The power you develop in skating comes from your hips down. Your hips and your behind must remain firm as you move along, not bobbing up and down with each stride. Leg action is bend and drive, bend and drive. Drive your legs as far out as they will go, then lift your skate just off the ice and back again for the next stride. Don't lift the skate too high off the ice; use a quick and sharp motion so there is no wasted time or effort.

In almost every case, this is the best way to get the most out of your skating. But one man who was different was Eddie Shack, a long-time player in the National Hockey League.

Eddie was a very powerful skater; he was bow-legged and he had his own style of skating. He was probably the only player in the history of hockey who could skate down the ice with a barrel between his legs and never miss a stride. He didn't bring his feet together as he moved along, and while this had always been his style, I don't recommend it for you. It takes a powerful man to skate this way and it would probably tire out most other people too fast.

The principle involved in skating backward is to maintain your balance. For an idea of correct position, imagine you are sitting in a chair with your knees bent and with your toes and your body held fairly straight. Your nose is out to about the front of your toes, and your behind is sticking out to the heels of your skates. The position is something like the letter "z."

While you put in work on your skating, it is well to also develop your stickhandling technique, which can be learned only by doing. You must learn to "feel" the puck with your stick so that you can keep your head up at all times while you cradle the puck for control. You cradle a puck by angling your stick over it a little.

Cradling the puck will also help you gain control of it if it is bouncing and rolling. If you leave the stick blade straight, the puck probably will hit it and bounce away.

PASSING

Whether you're pressing an attack or trying to get out of trouble, the best friend you may have on the ice is a sharp, accurate pass. The three fundamental prerequisites of a hockey player are skating, shooting, and passing, and no one who has ever played the game will underestimate the value of passing.

Putting the puck on a teammate's stick often can mean a goal. You may have only one inch in which to thread a pass, or perhaps even half an inch, but if you can deliver the puck to the right spot, the rival goaltender may be left without a chance to stop the ensuing shot.

How accurate must the pass be? Often, it must be precisely on the button. Your teammate may be well covered by a defensive player, and you may not be able to see any more than his stick on the ice. Still, it is your job to hit the stick. If you succeed only in putting the pass at your teammate's feet, by the time he gets it to his stick everyone else concerned, including the goaltender and the defensemen, has had time to react, and the play is lost.

At the other end of the ice, a good pass is essential to clear the puck out of your own zone, particularly if the opposition is persistent in its forechecking. Too often a team gets itself into trouble because the fellow with the puck makes a poor pass and the other side picks it up.

Before we get into a discussion of the actual passes themselves, it is important to note that the burden of passing doesn't all fall on the individual who initiates the play. There is someone on the other end who must receive the puck, and this isn't all as simple as it may seem.

In receiving a pass, your hands can't be too frozen or too tight around the stick. As the puck makes contact with the stick, you must ride with the impact of the puck, relaxing your grip somewhat on the stick so that the puck doesn't hit a hard, unyielding object and bounce away. This is the problem a lot of young players have when they first break into the NHL, caused partly, I suspect, by their own nervousness. The situation is similar to catching a baseball, when you don't just hold your hand out rigid, but instead move your hand on impact with the ball.

There are various types of passes a player is called upon to complete, ranging from the straight pass, in which two players are standing still, to moving passes. Then there is the matter of distance, where a pass may cover two feet or fifty feet or more, and the question of speed, where a player standing still may have to feed a teammate moving along at upward of twenty-five miles per hour, or instances where both players are in motion, either at the same speed or at varying speeds.

Timing and accuracy are all-important, and these are qualities that come only with practice. There are always decisions that must be made instantaneously upon releasing a pass. It can be hard, or soft, or fast, or you will have to decide whether to put the pass on your teammate's stick immediately or to lead him, such as a football quarterback does with a pass receiver.

If your teammate doesn't have too much clearance in front of him, and you don't know which way he may want to break, then you give him the puck as quickly as possible. However, if it's evident that he's about to beat the man defending against him, although he hasn't done it yet, then you lead him with the pass. In this event, the pass shouldn't be too hard; otherwise the intended receiver won't be able to get to it in time.

Much as in baseball, where a fielder aims his throw at a glove, in hockey the passer makes a teammate's stick his target. This is where the puck must wind up if the pass is to be successful. In leading a teammate with a pass, take into account how fast he is skating. If he is winging along at twenty-five miles per hour, you want to send that pass well enough in front of him so that he doesn't have to slow down, yet not so far ahead that he won't be able to reach it or that a defensive player will have a chance of getting there first.

In passing the puck, keep your head up and remain alert to changing situations so that you can change the direction of the pass, or its speed, until the very last moment. A little wrist action enables you to make any last-moment corrections.

There are no specific parts of the stick off which it is best to pass, although it is generally done in the center region of the blade.

Along with the more typical straight-ahead passes, we also have such variations as the flip pass and the drop pass. The flip pass can be done either on the forehand or backhand, and simply involves the lifting of the puck so it flips over the stick of a rival player who is between you and your intended receiver. When the puck lands back on the ice, it should lie flat so that your teammate can pick it up cleanly.

The flip pass requires a lot of practice to control, but once you are able to do it, it will become part of you. Not only will you be able to make accurate flip passes, but you'll also be able to control the speed.

A flip pass can be effected by cupping the puck, whereby you turn your stick down over it, then give it a little flip with your wrist; or, instead of cupping the puck, you can do it the opposite way by turning your stick out flat and applying a shoveling motion.

Flip passing is an art that youngsters should work on as much as possible during practice sessions. You can do this without the help of friends, too, by placing a two-by-four board on the ice, or even a stick, and passing over it, while you're standing still and while you're in motion. The results will be well worth the effort.

The drop pass is an enticing little devil; it looks very pretty when executed right, but is in reality a very dangerous pass that can create a lot of damage when it backfires. If you must drop a pass for a teammate, simply leave the puck where it is and let him skate up behind you to pick it up while you move ahead.

The temptation for many players is to put a tail on their drop passes, which is to say that they don't merely drop it, they give it a push as well. When this is done, the skater coming from behind to take the puck will skate right through it. And when this happens, you might have a situation where three players on your team are caught going the wrong way while an opposing player picks up the loose puck. Along with yourself, and the man for whom the drop pass was intended, the third forward in all likelihood was skating ahead toward the enemy goal.

It is so much simpler, and so much safer, to drop the puck where it lies and then try to take out the rival player in front of you while your teammate moves in from behind to take the puck.

After you've worked together with your teammates for a while, you can generally size up the situation and anticipate when a drop pass is likely. It isn't always helpful to announce it by shouting, because that also alerts the other team.

SHOOTING

I think that in this day our younger generation of athletes has come to realize that there are other essentials to winning games than hitting home runs, throwing touchdown passes, shooting baskets, and scoring goals. The glamor of a team game is shared just as much by those who stop the other guys from scoring as by those who do the scoring.

By the same token, there is no getting away from the fact that scoring runs or points or goals is essential for a winning effort, and in hockey one must be able to shoot the puck in order to survive. It isn't easy to shoot the flat disc both accurately and with power while it is sliding along on a slippery surface, as often as not while you are being knocked about by a rival player. But a team can't win without scoring, and you, as an individual, won't get very far in hockey without the ability to shoot.

Shooting is no longer confined to forwards, either. Eddie Shore, one of the great defensemen of all time, once said that the Boston management would fine him for scoring goals because as a defenseman it wasn't his job to shoot. Oddly enough, it was another Boston defenseman, Bobby Orr, who became the first of his breed to win an NHL scoring championship and thus bring to a fitting climax the revolution that hockey has undergone.

Shooting a puck is a precision task with subtle variations depending on the situation. There is a shot for all occasions, and the more adept you are at handling the stick the better your chances of surprising the defense and scoring goals. Just as a baseball pitcher who can mix 'em up with a variety of deliveries, a hockey player who can control his backhand along with his forehand has that much more firepower at his call.

Let's consider some of the variety of shots.

The first is an arm shot, on which you put everything you have behind it. This shot generally is taken at a medium-range distance from the net, anywhere from twenty-five to forty feet out.

The slap shot, popularized in recent years, usually is taken from farther out, although it can be used from anywhere and resembles a golf shot with its looping movement. The slap shot involves a windup, which gives the goaltender notice that it's coming, and some players, such as Bobby Hull, make it even more obvious by taking a big windup. Of course, even when a goaltender knows Hull is taking dead aim at him, the goaltender still can be hard-pressed to stop the bullet shot, which may be traveling at better than one hundred miles per hour. Bobby Orr is one of those who employs a short backswing, giving the goaltender less warning.

Slap shots are great crowd-pleasers because people all over the building can see them coming and then can anticipate the direct confrontation between shooter and goaltender.

A handicap of the slap shot is that it isn't as accurate as the wrist shot or the body shot, but it does come with more power behind it, and in its place it makes a nice addition to a well-equipped shooter's arsenal.

By contrast, the wrist shot comes with little or no warning, just a deadly snap of the wrist fired from close-in without hesitation. Even if the goaltender is aware that you've got good position and are almost certain to shoot, he doesn't know at what moment the shot will come, and since it is released so quickly he will have to be just as sharp to stop it.

Similar to the wrist shot is the snap shot, which also can be defined as a minislap shot. This again is accomplished with a snap of the wrists, but with the stick drawn back about an inch or two behind the puck. While with the wrist shot you don't draw your stick away from the puck, in using the snap shot you do move it back a fraction, but not nearly as far back as you would for a slap shot. This shot is employed generally from a twenty-to-thirty-foot range.

Gordie Howe used to be proficient with the wrist-snap shot, and it rubbed off on a long-time teammate of his, Alex Delvecchio, who also used it to good advantage.

The backhand is perhaps the toughest shot for players to score with, and it is virtually impossible to control with a curved stick. Too bad, because it's also a tough shot for the goaltender to handle. It is a deceptive shot, one you can hide with your body, and the goaltender doesn't seem to get as good a view of it as he does of forehanders.

How do you develop a variety of shots and learn how to use them? All it requires is practice, practice, practice. A simple word, and the answer to so many glorious dreams, but so difficult to follow through on.

Practice not only how to release the various shots, but also how to hit what you're aiming at. You can go in on the goaltender, take a good shot, and be beaten because he made the right move. You can also go in on the goaltender and beat yourself because you couldn't put the puck where the hole was. You put the shot into the goaltender instead of making him move for it.

This is what makes the difference between your supershooter and an average player. The good shooters direct the puck to the holes, not to the goaltender's body, and if the goaltender is going to beat them he's going to have to move and make a step.

Practice aiming at a small spot in the net, or even at the goalpost. If you're skating in and aiming at the goalpost, you should be able to hit it five of ten times.

A basic principle to remember is that if you're a left-hand shot, you should shoot off your right foot, and if you're a right-hand shot, you should shoot off your left foot. This will give you the proper balance.

Wrist action has a lot to do with lifting the puck off the ice when you shoot, as well as how you release it. If you want the puck to rise, angle the stick blade face upward as the puck leaves the stick on the follow-through instead of cradling it. To keep the puck on the ice, you cover or cradle it with your stick and you keep your wrists low and don't snap them on your motion.

MANEUVERABILITY

To my mind, no other sport calls on its participants to combine the need for brute strength with graceful guile as does ice hockey. Just how physically enervating the game is, is well illustrated by the short shift a line skates— about a minute and a half—before it is replaced by another. And yet the simple act of skating—without the body bumping and other physical contact—is an appealing art in itself, as witnessed by the growing popularity of figure skating.

Thus a good hockey player is not only one who is physically strong and can score goals, but also one who is able to skate with beautiful fluidity. And I don't mean only a fast skater, but one who possesses what I call maneuverability on the ice. This player is able to maneuver in any direction at any given moment, either forward, backward, sideways, or whichever. If he isn't able to do this, he is at a physical handicap and will not even be able to make full use of the skills he does have because a knowing rival will have cut off the lanes in which he can maneuver.

For example, if a defensive player knows that a certain player can't turn well to his left, he can anticipate with a certain degree of safety that his opponent will swing right in a given situation.

Rocket Richard was a man who could do just about anything on his skates, and as a result he was one of the toughest people in the world to stop when he came down his wing and cut for the net. He had tremendous cutting ability, great acceleration, thorough control of the puck, inborn instinct, a knowledge of what he wanted to do, and the talent to carry through with his plan.

Richard played the wrong wing—he was a left-hand shot on the right wing —and as he cut for the net he held his stick far over to one side with one hand, and with the other hand he'd hold off the defenseman. He was very strong, and as he came in there was no way for the defenseman to get around to his stick side once he had a stride advantage.

With most players, a defenseman can get in on the inside and dislodge the puck with his stick, or dislodge the puck on the outside by jostling the other player's stick enough so he'll lose control of the puck.

These ploys couldn't be worked on the Rocket. When you tried to go on the inside he'd hold your stick off with his free hand, because he was a left-hand shot. A right-handed shooter normally wouldn't have that hand free. If the defenseman tried to interfere with him by lifting Richard's stick off the ice and off the puck as well, Richard would just grab at it and hold it. If you tried to get him on the outside, as you went behind him he'd pull the puck across his body.

This meant the only thing a defenseman could do was to ride with the Rocket as long as possible, keeping his stick flat on the ice—perhaps holding on with just two fingers. When Richard got in front of the net, he always brought the puck over to the other side before shooting, and he would use both hands to shoot. This was about the only moment that a defenseman could risk a move.

When Richard started his motion of shooting, the defenseman would have to lift his stick and try to raise Richard's stick just enough so that it would be off the puck at that split second when he would have the goaltender beaten and an open net. By the time Richard got control of the puck again, he would have passed the net and be unable to score.

The point I've been trying to get across is not to extol the greatness of Rocket Richard, but to emphasize the qualities that make a great player. Not everyone can become a Rocket Richard, but you can make yourself adequate, or good, or even very good by rounding yourself into a complete hockey player.

The fewer weaknesses a player has, the more difficult it is for an opponent to stop him. A player who can move with as much fluidity to his left as to his right, who can stay on his feet and do his job while moving backward, is far more valuable than a teammate who can skate faster than he in a straight line, but who is unable to cut well to his left or wobbles while backstepping.

By the same token, it may seem glamorous to possess a bulletlike slap shot, but I'd prefer on my team someone who has only an adequate slap shot but who also can fool a goaltender with a quick wrist shot and can test the goaltender with a strong backhand.

Maneuverability means that a player can't be shut off simply by cutting off his favorite weapons. If you want an example of an all-around player, I can't think of a better one than Bobby Orr. There've been few players who could control the puck as he does, and he is a master at killing penalties simply by putting on a one-man skating show that is as graceful as any ballet. When an opponent moves into a corner to check him, Orr is just as likely to skate out to his left as to his right, and he appears to have a marvelous sense of anticipation that guides him to one side or the other.

While it's unquestionably more fun to do the things you do best, it is essential for a serious player to work on his weaknesses during practice sessions. During a game, when the pressure is on, it is only natural to turn to your strong suits so that you can play your best game. But it is important that in practice you try cutting to your wrong side, or to work on your backhander if it's noticeably weak.

If you don't strengthen your weak points, and instead continue to do the same things over and over in a game, you may get away with it for a while, but as you move up and the quality of your opposition improves, you will find yourself hopelessly overmatched.

There is nothing that can throw a rival off balance faster, and instill in him a great respect for you, than following this simple procedure: The first time you play against him, the first time you carry the puck, move around him to the right; the second time, try to cut by him on the left; and the third time, see if you can't just go right over the top of him.

Even if you can't carry through all the way, you'll have proven your maneuverability on ice, and that rival will remember that he can never anticipate which way you'll cut, meaning he'll have to allow you to make the first move. And never, never underestimate the value of being conceded the first move in such an explosive, quick-moving game.

FACEOFFS

A hockey game begins with the faceoff, and right off the bat you are faced with one of the more important moments of the game. There will be numerous faceoffs during a game, each critical in its own fashion because as long as you can control a faceoff you will maintain possession of the puck.

It's as simple as this: Possession of the puck means you are on offense. If you fail to get possession, it means you are on defense and in danger of being scored upon. I'd rather be on offense every time.

So important is the faceoff that some teams even have a specialist or two in this phase of the game, players who are inserted into the lineup just to control an important faceoff. Perhaps the best practitioner of this art in recent years has been Stan Mikita of Chicago.

Winning faceoffs requires quick reflex action and practice, sometimes hours a day on the faceoff itself. There are several principles that can be used as a guide, but these are meaningless unless you are willing to devote the necessary time to practice.

When you move into a faceoff circle, your whole being has to be at "go." From the moment you're in the circle, be very attentive to the linesman who is going to drop the puck, and by the time that puck leaves his hand, you should already be moving, just as if someone shot a gun to start a race. You can never be relaxed when you go in for a faceoff, and you must react instantaneously to the slightest movement. This principle, incidentally, applies to everyone on the ice at the time, a point I shall explain shortly.

The strategy of a faceoff is naturally contingent on the game situation and the position of play. A general plan would be to try to win the faceoff cleanly and go for a quick shot if you're deep in the other team's zone, but to be sure the other team doesn't win it if the faceoff takes place in your own end.

How do you prevent your rival from winning the faceoff in your own end? For him to win it, he has to get the puck and pull it back. You'll find that most players are able to pull it back better on their backhand than on their forehand, so you react accordingly to tie up the backhand.

It is up to the centerman to position his men around the circle, dependent on what strategy he plans to use. If the faceoff is in the other team's end, he may deploy his wingmen up on the line with the thought of drawing the puck back to a pointman (see Figure 1). Or he might pull one wingman just behind him at the edge of the circle toward the middle of the ice, from which

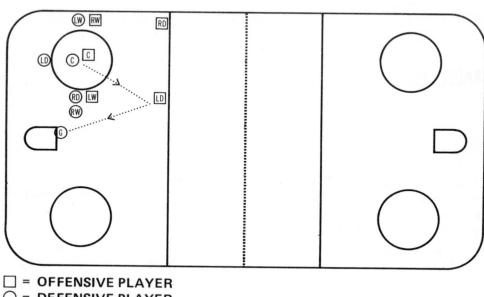

☐ = OFFENSIVE PLAYER
◯ = DEFENSIVE PLAYER
---- = PATH OF OFFENSIVE PLAYER
—— = PATH OF DEFENSIVE PLAYER
········· = PATH OF PUCK

Figure 1. Offensive right wing and left wing positioned on a straight line with faceoff. Offensive center wins draw and passes puck back to offensive left defenseman, who shoots on goal.

spot he can get an excellent shot if the centerman gets the puck back to him (see Figure 2).

If the two wingmen remain on the line, they will try to get in the way of the defensive players coming out, more or less interfering with them, so that the pointman will have an extra second or two in which to get off his shot.

A smart centerman will vary his plays, of course, unless he is sure he can beat a certain rival the same way all the time. Instead of drawing the puck back each time, the centerman may on occasion drive the puck straight for the net off a faceoff (see Figure 3). When this happens, one of his wingmen, knowing by some prearranged signal what is coming, bursts for the net. He may get there at the same time as the puck, with a chance of deflecting it at the last moment, or he may arrive there after the puck and be in position for a rebound.

As another change of pace, the centerman can try to pull the puck back on his forehand, rather than the backhand.

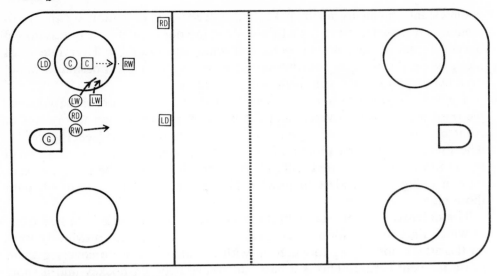

☐ = OFFENSIVE PLAYER
◯ = DEFENSIVE PLAYER
---- = PATH OF OFFENSIVE PLAYER
—— = PATH OF DEFENSIVE PLAYER
·········· = PATH OF PUCK

Figure 2.   Offensive right wing drops behind offensive center at edge of faceoff circle. Offensive left wing stays on line, blocking out defensive left wing from getting to offensive right wing until he can get shot away. Defensive right wing skates out to cover offensive left defensemen.

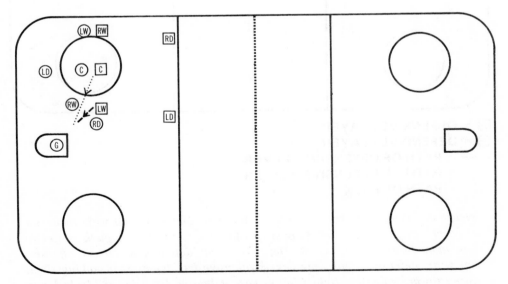

Figure 3.   Offensive center drives puck for goal, and offensive left wing bursts for net.

Quick movement by all five skaters, as well as anticipation by the goaltender, is just as necessary for a faceoff deep in your own end. It is easy to get burned by indecision, not knowing just what you must do. Everyone must move while the puck is still dropping to the ice from the linesman's hand, even before you know if your team will win or lose the draw.

The two wingmen race to the respective points to make sure those vulnerable positions are well covered, and the two defensemen station themselves in front of the net to defend against the opposition wingmen (see Figure 4). The two centermen, meantime, are one against one, the offensive centerman trying for a clean draw that will give his team possession, the defensive centerman doing his darndest to prevent his rival from carrying through with those plans.

The defensive players stay with their checks until the puck is turned over, at which time the situation is reversed, with the players who previously were on the attack now trying to catch up with the men who were covering them just a moment earlier. This is a basic difference between hockey and a sport

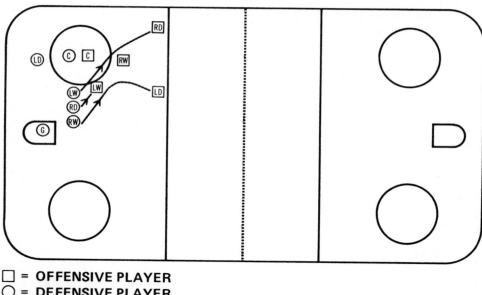

☐ = OFFENSIVE PLAYER
◯ = DEFENSIVE PLAYER
---- = PATH OF OFFENSIVE PLAYER
—— = PATH OF DEFENSIVE PLAYER
········ = PATH OF PUCK

Figure 4. Defensive center vs. offensive center: Defensive left wing races out to cover offensive right defensemen or offensive right wing if puck comes to him immediately from faceoff. Defensive right defenseman covers offensive left wing, defensive right wing covers offensive left defenseman, taking slight swing toward offensive right wing in case defensive left wing is blocked out. Defensive left defenseman covers offensive right wing as he moves toward goal.

such as football. In football, when a team loses the ball, it brings in the defensive squad, which concentrates solely on defense. In hockey, the same players are on offense one moment and on defense the next.

If a team is in its own half of the ice, but on the neutral side of the blueline, instead of trying to win the draw and gain possession, it may elect to drive the puck off the faceoff into the opposition's end. This is similar to a quick kick in football, with the team that shot the puck rushing in to get on top of the opposition before it can gain full control of the puck and form a play.

For a faceoff at center ice, there is no immediate danger of having a sudden goal scored against you. But if your side loses the draw, everyone must quickly pick up his man and backcheck. If you win the draw, try to bust away from your check so you have some skating room.

To set up this kind of a break, the centerman may have a wingman stand back a stride or two from the faceoff circle, then start to move just before the linesman releases the puck (see Figure 5). As the wingman picks up steam, the centerman will try to slap it through to him. This play requires intricate timing on the part of the centerman and wingman, and is predicated on the assumption that the centerman will win the draw cleanly.

With the center faceoff accomplished, the game is ready to proceed.

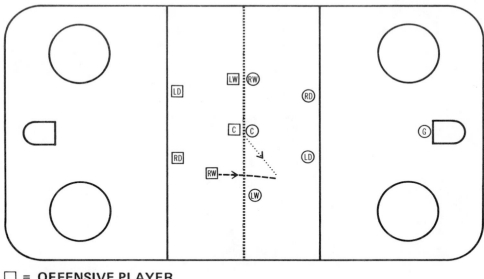

□ = OFFENSIVE PLAYER
○ = DEFENSIVE PLAYER
---- = PATH OF OFFENSIVE PLAYER
—— = PATH OF DEFENSIVE PLAYER
·········· = PATH OF PUCK

Figure 5. Offensive right wing gets under way just before puck is dropped. Offensive center slaps puck through to offensive right wing, who is on move while everyone else is caught standing.

OFFENSE WITH BOTH SIDES EVEN

There are six players to a side. Five of them are skaters—three forwards and two defensemen—who will move up and down the ice with the flow of play during their shifts. The sixth member of the team is the goaltender, who more or less remains glued to the one area just in front of his net.

During the course of action, both teams invariably will be penalized for rules infractions, causing them to skate shorthanded. When this happens, the team that has the extra man should have basic plays prepared and well practiced so that it can take full advantage of this added manpower. These plays will be discussed fully in later chapters, as will the best methods of defensing against the power play.

First, though, we will consider the more normal situation of play when both sides are even. But it should be thoroughly understood that even when both teams are at equal strength, the theories applicable to playing with an extra man should always be kept in mind. For even when there is no manpower difference, the offensive team—the one that is carrying the puck—should be looking for a way to break in past the defense, or to free a man, so that even for a moment the offense has the benefits of an extra man.

The game begins with the opening faceoff at center ice and, for the sake of illustration, we will say that your team winds up with the puck behind its own net. It is some 180 feet to the enemy goal, with five determined men patrolling the ice and doing their utmost to prevent you from testing their goaltender. What do you do now?

There are several means of formulating an attack, depending on the general system that a team employs. Just how you will carry the puck out of your own end also depends a great deal on just how much room the opposing team cares to give you. They may elect to move back toward center ice, picking up their checking assignments there, or they may forecheck so closely deep in your own end that you don't have time to set up a play.

When you are forced to make a quick play for safety's sake, just what this play will be is dependent on how your teammates are aligned. Because the rival team must deploy some of its men back in its own zone to prevent against a breakaway, members of the offensive team can relieve the pressure by skating back toward their own end and being available for a pass. Beware of a hasty pass, though. It doesn't take much of a mistake deep in your own end to turn on the red light for the other team.

Generally, a team will have enough time for a defenseman to pause for a moment or two behind his own net and size up the situation. In a situation such as this, some teams will play one defenseman behind the net and the other in front of it. The two wingmen will be over in the corners, with the centerman moving back deep.

At this point, if a forechecker enters the picture, the defenseman who is standing in front of the net should try to get in his way as much as possible, even if it means just standing his ground and forcing the would-be checker to take a stride or two around him. Often this extra second is all the other defenseman behind the net needs to make a good play.

The centerman, who is coming back toward his own net, can swerve either left or right, depending on his preference and the situation at hand. Whichever corner he chooses, the wingman manning that side will pull out just before the centerman gets there and will cut in toward the middle of the rink. Thus the wingman and the centerman have changed positions, in effect, with

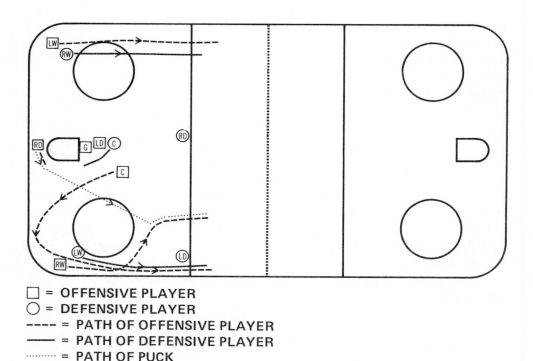

☐ = OFFENSIVE PLAYER
◯ = DEFENSIVE PLAYER
- - - - = PATH OF OFFENSIVE PLAYER
———— = PATH OF DEFENSIVE PLAYER
·········· = PATH OF PUCK

Figure 6. Offensive right wing receives pass as defensive left wing plays offensive center (in a zone defense, where player picks up attacker who comes into his area).

the wingman trying to pull his check with him toward the center. If the check doesn't go with him, the wingman will be clear to receive the pass from the defenseman and carry the puck toward center ice (see Figure 6). If the check pulls with the wingman, then the centerman moving into his position should be free for the pass (see Figure 7).

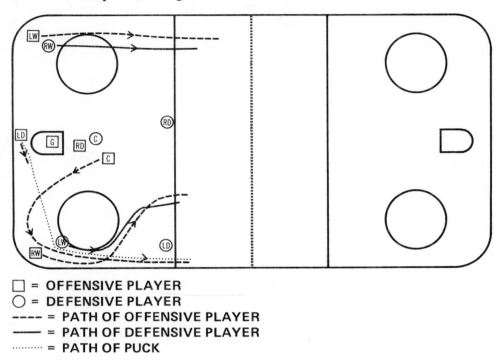

☐ = OFFENSIVE PLAYER
◯ = DEFENSIVE PLAYER
---- = PATH OF OFFENSIVE PLAYER
—— = PATH OF DEFENSIVE PLAYER
·········· = PATH OF PUCK

Figure 7. Offensive center receives pass as defensive left wing pulls with offensive right wing.

Another alternative for the defenseman standing behind the net, in addition to passing to a wingman or the centerman, would be to come out with the puck and then drop it back for his defensive partner, who is standing in front of the net (see Figure 8).

Through experience, the defenseman can read and interpret the situation before him instantaneously, judging, perhaps, if a rival player is edging into position to spring at him and disrupt the play. If the defenseman's teammates also are aware of the situation, they can drop back and help, so there will be little danger of losing the puck so disastrously close to their own goal.

Before we follow the puck across the center line, I would like to point out one further variance. Some teams prefer not to station one of their defensemen in front of the net, assigning him instead to one of the corners (see Figure 9). When this happens, the centerman, instead of falling back deep, will circle just inside the blueline, or sometimes just over it.

The defenseman behind the net will pass to his partner on the side, and he in turn will relay the puck to the centerman. Or the defenseman can carry the

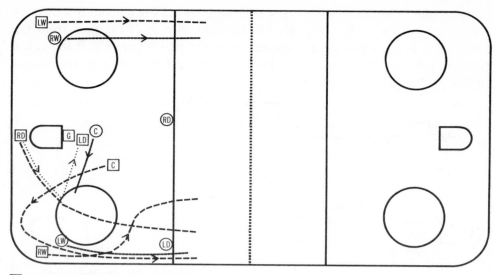

☐ = OFFENSIVE PLAYER
○ = DEFENSIVE PLAYER
---- = PATH OF OFFENSIVE PLAYER
—— = PATH OF DEFENSIVE PLAYER
········· = PATH OF PUCK

Figure 8. Offensive right defenseman drops puck back to his offensive left defenseman partner.

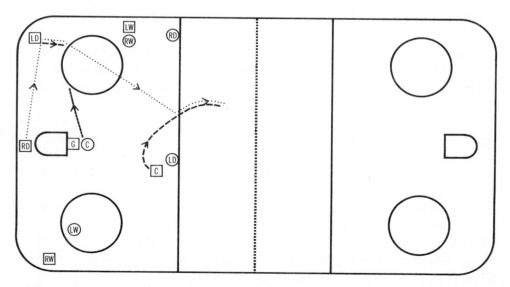

Figure 9. Offensive right defenseman behind goal passes to offensive left defenseman in corner. Defensive right wing picks up offensive left wing.

puck himself. The first pass from the deep defenseman is intended to beat the other team's centerman, should he be in forechecking. If a forechecking wingman also happens to be in deep, the defenseman can beat him with a pass to his own wingman (see Figure 10).

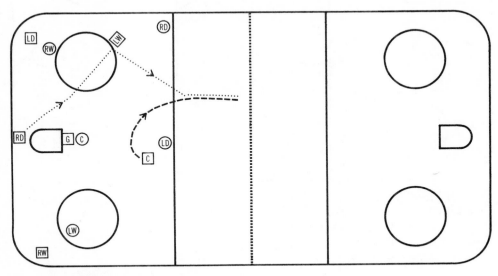

☐ = OFFENSIVE PLAYER
◯ = DEFENSIVE PLAYER
---- = PATH OF OFFENSIVE PLAYER
—— = PATH OF DEFENSIVE PLAYER
.... = PATH OF PUCK

Figure 10. One defenseman behind goal, one defenseman in corner checking. Defensive right wing picks up offensive left defenseman in corner. Offensive right defenseman passes puck to offensive left wing, who passes to offensive center.

Of course, there is an obvious inherent danger to the system of stationing one of your defensemen off to the side. If something goes wrong—and it does frequently enough to be considered—you have no one covering up in front of the net. I believe it is a wise practice to place a defenseman in front of his net when the puck is in your own zone. But some coaches, who feel their talent is good and their defensemen can handle the puck well, prefer to do otherwise.

Now we'll rejoin our wingman as he moves toward middle ice and receives a pass from his defenseman. As he does this, the wingman on the far side is moving quickly along the boards, and if the opposing defense stands up too far, or hesitates just a moment, he can be in and around them and in excellent position to attack should he receive a good lead pass (see Figure 11).

Even if he doesn't have a breakaway, your offense still is moving in the right direction and setting itself up for an attack on the net. As the forward

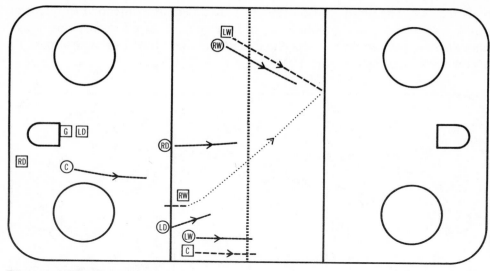

= OFFENSIVE PLAYER
= DEFENSIVE PLAYER
---- = PATH OF OFFENSIVE PLAYER
—— = PATH OF DEFENSIVE PLAYER
.... = PATH OF PUCK

Figure 11. Offensive right wing passes to offensive left wing, who is behind defensive right defenseman and has also a one-step advantage on defensive right wing.

line hits the blueline, they can choose from a number of plays, depending again on the situation—whether any member is free, if they're being closely checked, if they have a three-on-one or a three-on-two break, or whatever. A later chapter is devoted exclusively to the handling of breakaways, so we will confine ourselves for now to dealing with a tight-checking situation.

The forward with the puck can either carry it on his own or pass to an open wingman, who can cut for the net. The other wingman should also break for the net once the puck has been advanced that far, with the center-man dropping back into the slot, about twenty-five feet straight out from the net, where he serves as a safety valve as well as a member of the attacking unit (see Figure 12). Or, if the centerman goes in deep, that second wingman can move into the slot.

If something goes wrong—a bad pass, a deflection, a rebound flying onto the stick of an opposing player—the centerman is in position to pick up a

Facing Page: *Figure 12. Offensive center carries puck across blueline as defensive right defenseman and defensive left defenseman back up, enabling both offensive left wing and offensive right wing to break for goal. Offensive center stops in slot (twenty-five feet out) and is safety valve. Offensive center either passes to offensive left wing or offensive right wing or elects to shoot.*

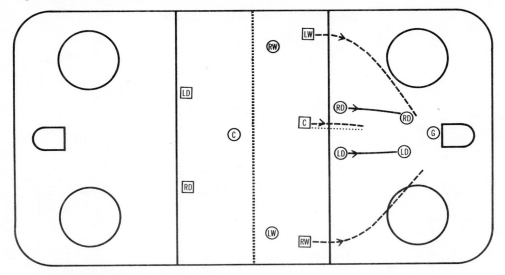

☐ = OFFENSIVE PLAYER
◯ = DEFENSIVE PLAYER
---- = PATH OF OFFENSIVE PLAYER
—— = PATH OF DEFENSIVE PLAYER
·········· = PATH OF PUCK

check going the other way. If all three forwards crowd around the net, once the puck gets beyond them they'll all be caught behind the play, and the opposition will be in excellent position for a breakaway (see Figure 13). With the centerman back in the slot, he's a precaution against this possibility, and he's also in position to join the attack. It's much easier to move forward two or three strides to pick up a puck than it is to backtrack.

Should the puck come out to the centerman, either through a pass or some other means, he is in a tremendous vantage point to take a shot. There are very few better places to beat a goaltender from than twenty to twenty-five feet out and a position directly in front of him.

There's another good reason for the centerman to avoid the front of the net. If all three forwards are bunched close to one another, it is that much easier for the defense to cover them all. With the centerman in the slot, one of the defensemen will have to leave the front of the net to cover him. That's going to leave one wingman, and perhaps both, wide open in front of the net.

Passing the puck is perhaps your greatest aid in moving up ice and setting yourself up for the attack. Of course, if a man is clear and he is an adept stickhandler, there's no reason he can't change the pattern and carry the puck himself. But generally a few crisp passes make the way so much easier.

If you transfer the puck from center to wing, it changes the picture for the defense, and they have to change their strategy. Then if the puck comes back to center, the defense has to reform itself once again. This is much like a

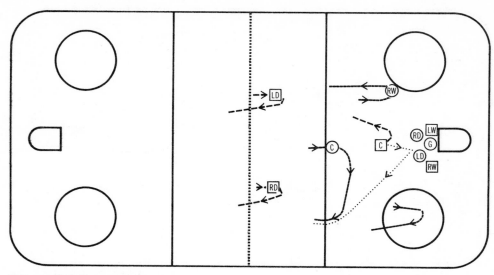

☐ = OFFENSIVE PLAYER
○ = DEFENSIVE PLAYER
---- = PATH OF OFFENSIVE PLAYER
—— = PATH OF DEFENSIVE PLAYER
········· = PATH OF PUCK

Figure 13. Offensive center's shot blocked by defensive left defenseman, rebounds out to backchecking defensive center, who goes on offensive. Defensive right wing and defensive left wing immediately go with defensive center, trapping offensive left wing and offensive right wing in deep. Offensive center must turn and pick up either defensive left wing or defensive right wing to prevent a three-on-two break against his team. Offensive left defenseman and offensive right defenseman reverse direction when they see puck change hands.

quarterback throwing the defense off stride by passing the football behind the line of scrimmage.

The defensemen, once they have initiated the offensive play deep in their own end, are also an integral part of the attack and should be utilized as such. You have a five-man unit out there, and the team should move as five men.

Although they are trailing the play, the defensemen should follow it as closely as possible and move as fast as they can inside the other team's blueline. Once there, they take up the position known as the points—some five to ten feet inside the blueline and alongside the two boards (see Figure 14) or one toward the middle of the ice and the other at the boards (see Figure 15). Quite often, the pointmen are the key to the whole attack.

If one of the forwards is checked or tied up in the corner, he can throw the puck back to a pointman. The pointman, in turn, has numerous alternatives.

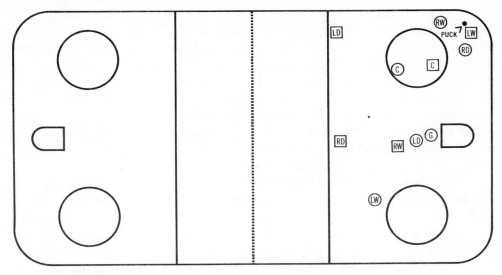

□ = OFFENSIVE PLAYER
○ = DEFENSIVE PLAYER
---- = PATH OF OFFENSIVE PLAYER
—— = PATH OF DEFENSIVE PLAYER
········· = PATH OF PUCK

Figure 14. Puck in offensive left-hand corner. Offensive left defenseman plays along boards inside blueline; offensive right defenseman plays near middle of ice inside blueline.

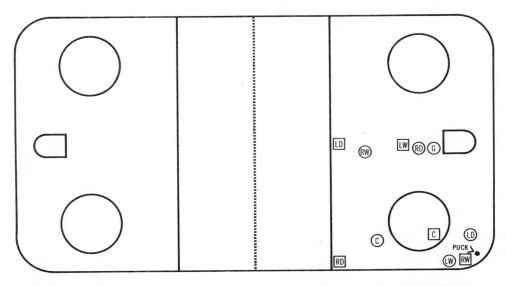

Figure 15. Puck in offensive right-hand corner. Offensive left defenseman plays near middle of ice inside blueline; offensive right defenseman plays along boards inside blueline.

He can shoot the puck himself (see Figure 16)—and his shot can be ex-
tremely dangerous, particularly if the goaltender is screened by a mass of
bodies—or he can pass across to his defensive partner on the other point (see
Figure 17), thus causing the entire defense, as well as the goaltender, to shift
their focus from one side of the ice to the other. And, of course, the pointman
also can pass the puck to any of his forwards in the middle who happen to be
free, or back into the corner to the original passer.

The pointmen are always on the alert for a sudden change of fortune that
sees the other team wind up with the puck. By working together, and maintaining proper position, the pointmen shouldn't be trapped.

If the play happens to be formulating on the left side, the left pointman
should be prepared to move in a little closer in case he can be of any help to
his forwards, while the right pointman should back up a stride or two over
the blueline and toward the middle of the rink (see Figure 18). In this way,
he'll be ready to move back if the other team gets the puck, while at the same
time he need move forward only a stride or two to get back over the blueline
and rejoin the attack if the play moves to his side of the ice or his team
regains control of the puck.

Again, as we mentioned earlier in this chapter, it is much easier to move in
a stride or two than it is to have to back up and then try to catch someone on
a breakaway.

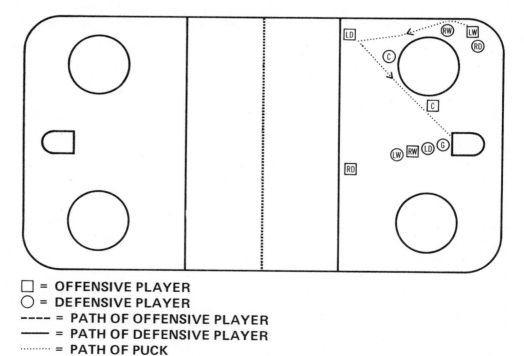

☐ = OFFENSIVE PLAYER
○ = DEFENSIVE PLAYER
---- = PATH OF OFFENSIVE PLAYER
—— = PATH OF DEFENSIVE PLAYER
········· = PATH OF PUCK

*Figure 16. Offensive left wing passes back to pointman, the offensive left
defenseman, who shoots at goal. Offensive center has chance to deflect or
screen goalie or pounce on rebound. Offensive right wing has same opportunity.*

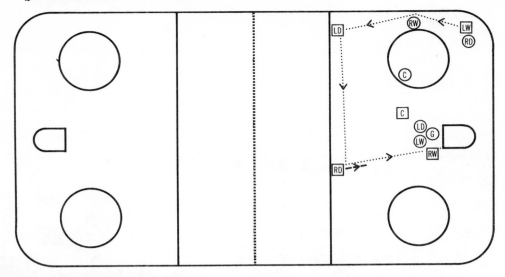

□ = OFFENSIVE PLAYER
○ = DEFENSIVE PLAYER
---- = PATH OF OFFENSIVE PLAYER
——— = PATH OF DEFENSIVE PLAYER
········· = PATH OF PUCK

Figure 17. Offensive left wing passes to offensive left defenseman, who passes to offensive right defenseman, who carries puck a few feet toward goal and then shoots. Offensive right wing is screening goaltender and tying up defensive left wing. Offensive center is a decoy and causing disturbance and is ready to pounce on any rebound.

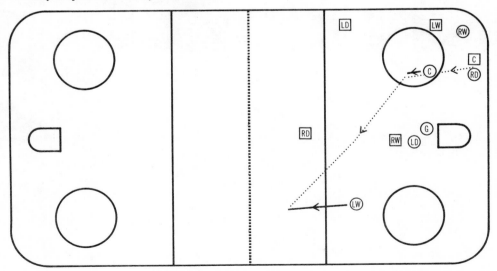

Figure 18. Offensive center and defensive right defenseman are fighting for puck control. Puck slips out to defensive center, who takes a couple of steps and passes to defensive left wing, who is breaking up ice fast. If offensive right defenseman stays in too deep, he will be unable to get back in time to defend against defensive left wing.

THE POWER PLAY

The power play is the most potent offensive weapon in hockey aside, perhaps, from the rarely called penalty shot, and should be understood thoroughly to make it succeed on the ice.

In its basic form, a penalty called on a player for any one of numerous infractions allows the opposing team to skate with a one-man advantage for two minutes. Occasionally, a team can find itself with a two-man advantage, but we'll concentrate here on the more normal situation in which one team has five skaters and the other team four.

The team with the extra skater has a tremendous advantage, but because the short-handed team is concentrating solely on defense and has the privilege of icing the puck without drawing a whistle, the attacking unit must be well organized and aware of what it is trying to do before it can succeed in scoring a goal.

There are three basic stages in setting up your play. The first is to get the puck out of your own end, the second is to get it into the opposition's end, and the third is to gain or keep possession in the offensive zone.

Too often a power play is ineffective because the team carrying the puck down ice is checked at the opposition's blueline and the puck is cleared all the way back into its own end. Keep in mind that you have a whole two minutes in which to take advantage of the penalty, and it isn't necessary to speed things up from the outset and forgo organization.

A pointman should be familiar to most of you as the player who stands just inside the enemy's blueline while a power play is under way, firing the long bullets at the goalie and protecting the puck from getting back across the blueline. A pointman also performs some other vital functions, albeit less spectacular, in getting the power play started.

Quite often a pointman will go behind his own net with the puck and just pause, realizing it is better to take an extra moment or two to set up an attack than it is to rush headlong up ice.

One effective way of getting the play started is for the centerman to swing around behind the net and take the puck from the pointman (see Figure 19).

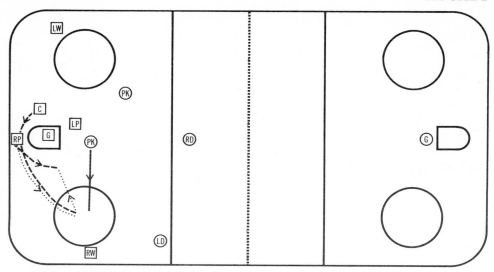

= OFFENSIVE PLAYER
= DEFENSIVE PLAYER
---- = PATH OF OFFENSIVE PLAYER
—— = PATH OF DEFENSIVE PLAYER
········· = PATH OF PUCK

Figure 19. Offensive right pointman stops behind net with puck. Offensive center skates in and picks up puck on the fly and starts up ice when defensive penalty killer cuts him off. Offensive center drops puck to offensive right pointman, who either carries puck or passes puck to offensive left wing, depending on what second penalty killer does.

If the opposing team's forechecker sticks with him, the center can drop it right back to the pointman who is trailing the play, and he has the option to continue carrying the puck himself or make a return pass to a forward.

An alternative play is for an offensive wingman to go back into a corner on either side of his own net, make a turn, and then start up ice just as the pointman begins to make his move (see Figure 20). It's generally easy to beat an incoming checker if the pointman pulls the defensive player to him by holding the puck, then hits his winger with a good pass just after he's started moving.

The wingman then only has to worry about a second defensive player, and if this player is moving in he can easily be overcome if the attacking team has formulated its plan well. It will have the center skating up in his position, and possibly the other winger, so that the wing with the puck can pass either to his center or the other winger on the far side.

In any case, however, you come out of your own end, and it's a matter of working together as a unit and knowing the capabilities of each of your teammates. Some teams will keep one of its pointmen in front of its net until the attack is well under way to act as a precautionary guard in case the other

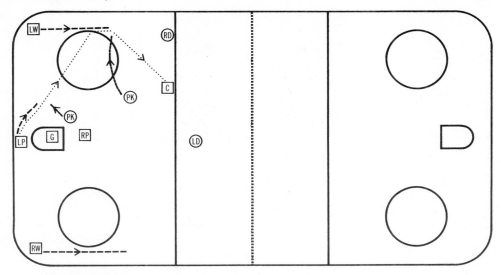

= OFFENSIVE PLAYER
= DEFENSIVE PLAYER
---- = PATH OF OFFENSIVE PLAYER
—— = PATH OF DEFENSIVE PLAYER
·········· = PATH OF PUCK

Figure 20. Offensive left pointman carries puck a few steps and then passes to offensive left wing, who carries puck a few strides and passes to offensive center. Offensive right wing is moving up ice fast and should be open.

team steals the puck, and also to serve as a mobile block who will force the incoming checker to take a wider berth. This gives the man behind the net a better opportunity to start his play.

How the play is started is important, and it is also important when you come out of your own end that it is not being left to just one man to make the play, but that the whole unit is moving up ice together. Too many power plays are ruined because only one man is skating at the start of the attack, and his teammates are lagging behind the play or going the other way. Everyone must have a sense of direction and must move together.

As the attacking team moves closer to the other team's blueline, it will meet stiffer resistance. It is not always a simple matter to get the puck over the blueline, and again it is best to have an idea of what you are trying to do.

The defense may be playing four men across, stationing its two forwards and two defensemen near the blueline. In that case, one of the attacking wingmen, instead of going over the blueline, can cut toward the center of the rink just at the blueline, making sure he stays onside. This winger then can move in the way of the defenseman who is waiting there to check the oncoming puckcarrier (see Figure 21).

If the puckcarrier has elected to continue with it himself, rather than pass off, he might cut to the outside position that his wingman has just left. If that

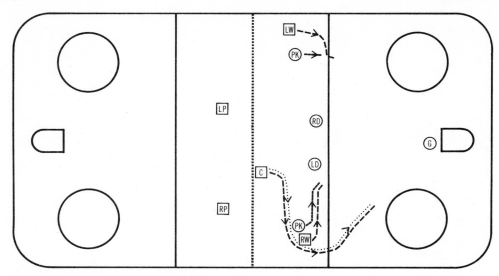

= OFFENSIVE PLAYER
= DEFENSIVE PLAYER
---- = PATH OF OFFENSIVE PLAYER
——— = PATH OF DEFENSIVE PLAYER
········· = PATH OF PUCK

Figure 21. Offensive right wing cuts toward middle of ice, pulling defensive penalty killer with him and also blocking defensive left defenseman from getting to offensive center as he cuts through hole left as a result of offensive right wing's move. Key to play: Both offensive left wing and offensive right wing must not cross blueline until offensive center has moved puck over blueline.

wingman had made his move properly, he would have drawn a defensive pointman and winger toward the middle of the ice, leaving his former position unprotected. The key to this play is that the two offensive wingmen stay onside by not going over the blueline until the puck does.

Sometimes you just can't penetrate a stacked defense by finding an opening through which to carry the puck or with a pass, in which case you simply send the puck into one of the corners and then race in to try to gain clear possession or else to tie up the puck and get a whistle.

The key to making this happen is teamwork. Everyone on the offensive team should have been moving together, and in the same direction, since the play's inception instead of having one man going forward, another standing still, and someone else moving backward.

It is then up to the puckcarrier to make his play before his teammates are forced to stop at the blueline or risk going offside. In other words, if they're skating along at thirty miles an hour and the puckcarrier hasn't sent the puck across the blueline by the time his teammates reach that point, they'll have to slow down or stop altogether, thus losing their momentum.

However, if they can continue across the blueline without a losing a stride, they'll have an excellent chance of retrieving the puck off the boards before the defensive team, which had been grouped at the blueline, can backtrack. Even if the offensive player doesn't reach the puck first, chances are he'll still be quick enough to tie up the defenseman who beat him to it, thus calling for a faceoff deep in enemy territory.

Should an attacking player approach the blueline and see that he's slightly ahead of the puck, he should turn and cut along the line, keeping one foot onside. Merely dragging a foot for a split second will make the play onside.

Occasionally, to add a twist to your attack and confuse the defense, one of the players can skate ahead of the play and stop just before the blueline. The puckcarrier then will throw a quick pass to him, and he'll receive it with his feet in neutral ice, but with his stick over the blueline. This means that the puck also will be over the blueline, and every man is free to charge into the defensive team's zone. Once this is accomplished, great pressure is thrown on the defensive unit, because any one of the attackers can go straight toward the net, and if nobody picks him up he's wide open for a pass and a clear shot.

Examining this defense-busting play from another view, consider that you're the puckcarrier flying down center ice and you have a wingman who's ahead of the play, waiting at the blueline. The defense is focused on you, with at least two of their four skaters looking to check you, and you know that your wingman is left unguarded in front of you. Flip the puck to him, perhaps a foot or two just over the line and along the boards. When he receives the puck, the whole picture has changed for the defense.

Instead of you carrying the puck down center ice, the puck is already over the line and to a far side of the rink. The defense suddenly has to reverse itself and chase after the puckcarrier. This leaves you free to continue steaming down the center for a possible return pass after the defense was drawn off to the side (see Figure 22). If you do get the return pass, then the second defenseman will be drawn to you and leave an opening for your other wingman on the far side or your other pointman to come down the middle.

However you handle it, this play opens up the defense and gives you a good shot to capitalize on your one-man advantage.

Once the offensive team has possession of the puck in the enemy zone, it should be able to turn on the pressure and pepper the goalie with at least several good shots. You won't score all the time you have a man advantage, but if you make the right plays you will get on the scoreboard a satisfactorily proportionate number of times.

To make the power play work, it is essential to keep the puck inside the offensive zone and to prevent the defensive unit from getting a clear chance to send the puck back over the blueline.

Since the attacking team has the extra man, it normally should send two men after the puck if it loses control. One man should take the defensive player out with his body, while the second man picks up the puck. Even if the defensive player is able to take a poke at the puck, if he is hemmed in by two opponents, chances are his clearing attempt won't have much steam behind

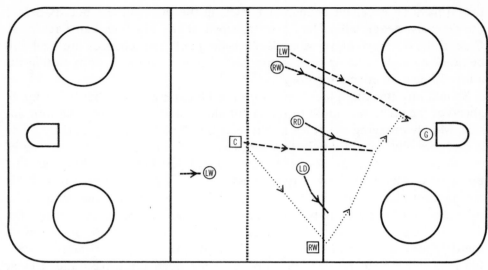

☐ = OFFENSIVE PLAYER
◯ = DEFENSIVE PLAYER
---- = PATH OF OFFENSIVE PLAYER
——— = PATH OF DEFENSIVE PLAYER
·········· = PATH OF PUCK

Figure 22.   Offensive center passes to offensive right wing just over offensive blueline, then bursts between defensive left defenseman and defensive right defenseman and receives return pass from offensive right wing. Defensive right defenseman is forced to try to check offensive center, so offensive center passes puck to onrushing offensive left wing, who has beaten his check.

it, and one of the offensive pointmen might be able to prevent the puck from going over the blueline.

This brings us back to those all-important pointmen. Earlier in this chapter I discussed their importance in initiating the power play. Now I would like to cover another facet of their job.

A pointman must have a great shot, he must be able to make quick and accurate passes, and he must be able to react to a situation instantaneously, sensing whether he should take a shot, make a pass, or stickhandle around a man coming toward him. The pointman is also the last line of defense for his team (except, of course, for the goaltender) should the other team get the puck, and if he makes a mistake, such as shooting or passing the puck so that an enemy forward can pick it off, the opposition can suddenly get a breakaway. And one of the most demoralizing things that can happen to a hockey team is to allow a short-handed goal.

A pointman should size up the situation even before he receives the puck so he can make his move without a moment's pause. If he elects to make a pass, it must be accurate. The idea is to keep the puck moving quickly until it gets to the man who is unguarded and in good position to shoot, so if the pass is off target it might take the intended receiver an extra second or two to get control of it. This slows down his momentum and gives the defensive team a chance to recover.

After making his pass, the pointman might bust into a hole himself in anticipation of a return pass. This is an effective means for the pointman to get around a defensive forward who was sent out to check him.

Most penalty-killing teams are told that a pointman should be allowed only one shot, if he can get it away. But the defensive player is cautioned against allowing the pointman to skate around him and pick up a return pass, because if the pointman succeeds in this, it's trouble for the defensive team.

Another member of the power-play team should be stationed in front of the net, tying up the other team's defensemen, screening their goaltender, and in general causing a lot of commotion out there. Not the least benefit of a strong man who can hold his ground is the chance to pick up quick passes or stray rebounds for easy shots.

A big man such as Jean Beliveau was always very dangerous in front of the net, with a lovely knack for deflecting shots past the goaltender.

It is generally best for a pointman to keep his long shots low, either on the ice or just two or three inches off it, so that one of his teammates in front of the net might be able to deflect it. Even if there is no deflection, a low shot is very dangerous and hard to handle. The goaltender not only has to worry about making the save, but also controlling the rebound as well. If it's a waist-high shot, or any shot high enough for the goaltender to catch, there is no rebound. He just holds it and the play is dead.

But if the shot is along the ice where the goaltender has to make a foot save or a leg save, there's going to be a rebound, and frequently he's in no position to recover from the first stop and turn back a rebound shot.

Another factor in favor of the low shot is that it's the toughest for a defenseman to block. A player who gets hit on the ankle bone or the toe cap of the skate is going to feel it, and he's going to get a little leery of putting his body in front of those shots. Should a defenseman still risk it, he doesn't have as much equipment below his knees as above it with which to catch a piece of the puck. His body is much wider up higher, and he has his pants, his gloves, his shoulder pads, hip pads, and thigh pads to make him that much bulkier. A defenseman can throw his body in front of a shot, but it requires exact timing. Otherwise it can be a dangerous play, for if he misses, or is fooled, he's off his feet and can't react as fast to the next play. When he does block the shot, it's a good play.

If there is too much of a traffic jam in front of the net, the pointman might feel it too risky to send the puck into the middle of a melee. Instead, one of his forwards, aware of the situation, can direct himself to the fringe of the pileup, perhaps a step or two from the goal. The pointman then will slide a quick pass to him right alongside the throng, and when he gets the puck it may be just a case of tipping it into the net.

Of course, not everyone is going to score on a power play, and not everyone should concentrate only on positioning himself in a spot from which he can

get a good shot. For example, a player should consider when he can best serve as a shield for the puckcarrier. Simply by standing still, or moving just a stride or two, he might be able to prevent a defensive man from getting to the puckcarrier.

In attempting to use yourself as a block, remember that you're not permitted to take out or interfere with anyone, *but*, at the same time, there is the question of who's interfering with whom. If you are standing your ground, there's no cause for an interference call, and by doing so you force the defensive player to take an extra stride or two to get around you while your teammate carrying the puck has that added advantage in setting up a play or taking his shot.

On occasion, a team will find itself on the long end of a two-man advantage. This presents an excellent chance to score, although many opportunities have been lost simply through overeagerness.

When you have an advantage of five men to three, the primary concern is to gain possession of the puck and move it into the other team's zone. Then pass the puck around until you pull a defensive player out of position so that you'll end up with a man directly in front of the net.

Since you can score only one goal on each penalty, you can afford to invest a few seconds of time in organizing your attack and making a few passes until a man is open in good scoring position.

Summing up briefly what we have discussed in this section, the essence of an effective power play is to move the puck over the other team's blueline and to keep control of it in their end. Position your men properly, with the two pointmen at their respective stations along the two sideboards and a strong player in front of the net where he can tie up at least one and perhaps two defensemen while creating general havoc in that vital area.

To me, the key to creating serious scoring threats is crisp, quick passing to pull one of the defensive players out of position, and constant movement by the attacking team. A man who remains stationary, waiting for the play to come to him, is easy to watch and to defend against. But if a man is on the move, he's here one moment and gone the next. He disrupts the defensive pattern, and if they don't react quickly enough he can bust into a hole and set himself up for a good shot. A fine example of this type of player is Yvan Cournoyer of Montreal.

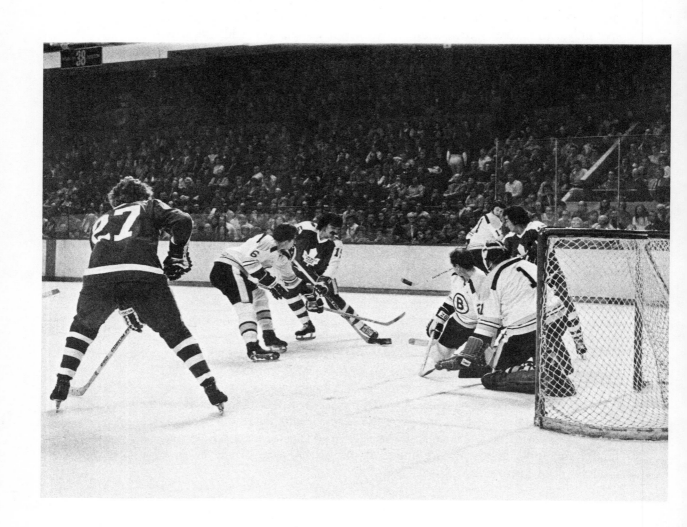

DEFENSING THE POWER PLAY

While it may appear more glamorous to be a member of your team's power play, most good players realize that just as many games are won by the penalty-killing unit, and it requires just as skillful an operative to kill the penalty when his team is short-handed as one who can capitalize on a power play.

It is important not to lose sight of your objective when you are skating one man, or possibly two men, short. Your main aim is to kill the penalty for the full two minutes, or whatever duration it may be, to prevent the other team from scoring.

When your team is playing four skaters against five and the play moves into your end of the ice, the accepted procedure is to move into what is called a box position (see Figure 23). The two defensemen stay in front of the net while the two forwards (who often are the specialists on the team in killing penalties) form the other points of the box, one stationing himself in front of the offensive team's pointman and the other in front of the second pointman.

The box, of course, will vary in size, depending on what the attacking team does, and can be stretched wider or closed tighter. If someone busts into the middle of the box, it can be pulled shorter to check that man (see Figure 24). If the puck comes out to the pointman on the left side, then the defensive man covering the right-side pointman may pull back into the middle of the box. Should the left pointman pass cross ice to the right pointman, then the left defensive forward will skate back to cover him, and the right defensive forward will pull in and cover the man in the slot (see Figure 25).

There are two prime objectives the short-handed team should keep in mind. First, keep the offensive team on the outside of that box, and second, clear out immediately any attackers who try to position themselves in front of your net.

The man who is allowed to position himself in front of the net is a triple threat. He can deflect a shot by a teammate, putting the goaltender in a helpless position to defend himself; he can also pounce on a rebound for another easy shot; or he can screen the goaltender.

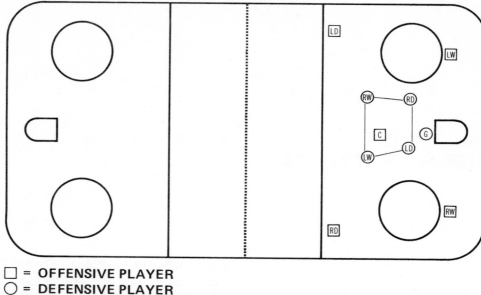

= OFFENSIVE PLAYER
= DEFENSIVE PLAYER
---- = PATH OF OFFENSIVE PLAYER
—— = PATH OF DEFENSIVE PLAYER
·········· = PATH OF PUCK

Figure 23.   Defensive unit killing penalty in own end plays box defense.

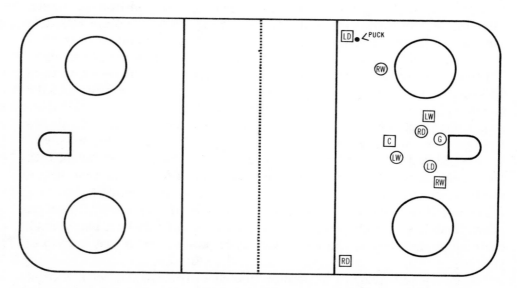

Figure 24.   Offensive left defenseman has puck and is being covered by defensive right wing. Defensive left wing has tightened box by pulling into middle of ice to cover offensive center.

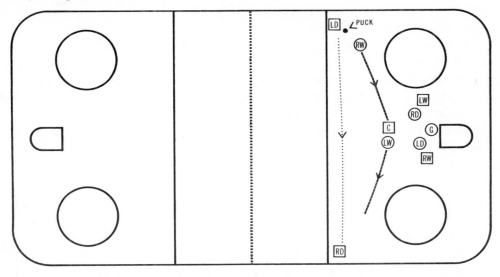

Figure 25. Offensive left defenseman passes to offensive right defenseman. Defensive left wing leaves offensive center to check offensive right defenseman. Defensive right wing leaves offensive left defenseman to cover offensive center in slot. Defensive right defenseman covers offensive left wing, and defensive left defenseman covers offensive right wing.

If the two prime objectives just mentioned are accomplished and the point-man elects to pierce your defensive box by shooting from the outside, it is generally best to allow the goaltender to handle the shot. The defensemen should make certain there is no one in the vicinity who can deflect that shot, and they must be ready to pounce on the rebound, or at least prevent an opponent from getting to it near the net.

A short-handed team can't afford to tie up one of its men on one attacker, unless he feels he can freeze the puck. The other team still would have an extra skater, so you can't afford to lose one of your men from the play. It is more important to play the puck and try to clear it the length of the rink.

Bob Goldham, a tall, rangy defenseman who used to play for Detroit, was perhaps the best at blocking shots by dropping his body in front of them. Bob wasn't the fastest skater, but he had an uncanny knack of making his move at the precise moment and falling on the puck.

The timing on this play is most important. You have to be certain the player is going to shoot, and once he's committed himself, you must make your move in a flash. If you fall too soon, the player with the puck can simply go around you instead of shooting, and be clear for an even better shot.

Another caution about dropping to the ice to block shots is that you may very well succeed—but with your head. A good many players have been conked on the head in such a situation, and some have been badly hurt.

On rare occasions, your team may find itself two men short, playing three skaters against five. By all means, this is a critical situation, but it needn't be

fatal. Keep cool, concentrate on defense only, know what you're trying to ac-
complish, and you can survive.

The three men on the defensive unit should position themselves in a triangle, two men in front of the net and the other forming the point in front of
and between them (see Figure 26). Again, the idea here is to prevent the attacking team from getting a clear shot from a position directly in front of the
goaltender. If you're going to yield a shot, let it be from an angle so your
goaltender can move to cut down that angle and have a better chance of
making the save.

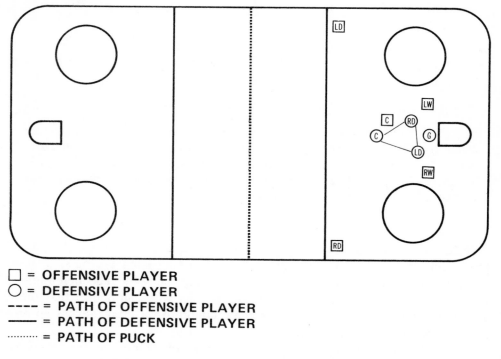

☐ = OFFENSIVE PLAYER
○ = DEFENSIVE PLAYER
---- = PATH OF OFFENSIVE PLAYER
—— = PATH OF DEFENSIVE PLAYER
·········· = PATH OF PUCK

Figure 26.   Two men short—play triangle defense.

There are two principal ways of maintaining the triangle position when a
team is two men short. In the first, the man who is at the point of the triangle
flows with the tide of play, shifting to his right if the puck goes to the offensive team's left point, and overbalancing to his left if the play is on the other
side (see Figure 27). But he must be careful not to pull over too far to one
side, or else he won't be able to get back to prevent either pointman from
busting in on the net.

A less frequently used defensive measure can be triggered if, for example,
the man at the point of the triangle is shaded near the offensive left pointman.
If that pointman should send the puck cross ice to the right pointman, then
the defensive unit simply changes position. This means that the defenseman
on the left side skates out to meet the right pointman who now has the puck.
Meantime, the other two defensive players also are switching positions (see
Figure 28). This move is made because it allows the man closest to the puck-

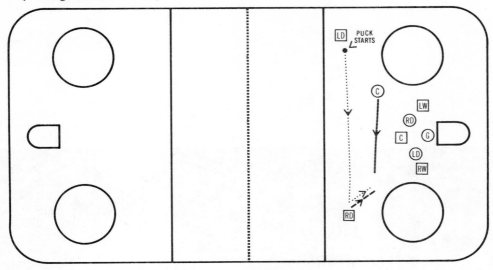

Figure 27. Offensive left defenseman passes puck to offensive right defenseman, who carries puck toward goal to shoot or pass. Defensive center tries to cross ice to check offensive right defenseman. Defensive right defenseman and defensive left defenseman are trying to check offensive left wing, offensive right wing, and offensive center. Offensive center is most dangerous, as he is in slot. Goalie will play one man, too, preferably man at side of net.

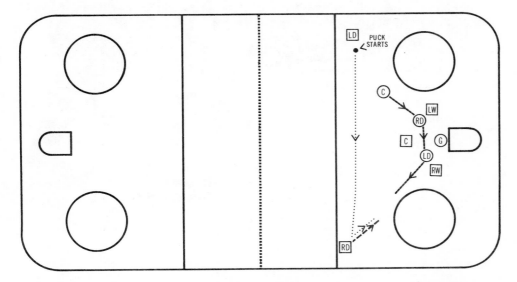

Figure 28. Offensive left defenseman passes puck to offensive right defenseman, who carries puck toward goal to shoot or pass. Defensive center rushes back to cover offensive left wing and offensive center. Defensive right defenseman crosses over to cover offensive center and offensive right wing. Defensive left defenseman moves out to cover offensive right defenseman. Offensive center is most dangerous, as he is in slot. Goalie will play one man, too, preferably man at corner of net, either offensive right wing or offensive left wing.

carrier to cover that player.

Whether your team is short one man or two, tight teamwork is of the essence if you are to escape without allowing a goal. You have to work as a unit, and you have to talk to one another. If a teammate gets the puck and you're in the slot, let him know where you are, or if he comes out of the corner with the puck and there's someone on his tail, let him know whether he can dump the puck along the boards to you or whether he can break clear himself.

No one I've ever known had eyes behind his head, but many a time I've seen a player "lend" his eyes to a teammate who didn't have a split second to spare to turn his head around. Everyone should help each other. You are a team, and you must work as a team.

DEFENSE WITH BOTH SIDES EVEN

The sooner you can apply pressure on the team with the puck, the better are your chances to break up the play before it reaches your own zone. You can also risk being a little more chancy when the puck is still a long distance from your goal.

By applying pressure as soon as the other team gets the puck, you might be able to upset their pattern before they can gain full control and organize their attack. The puck may still be in a corner, or hugging the boards, or alongside the net, and if you can move in, then you may be able to tie up the player and get a faceoff or, if one of your teammates is with you, you might be able to force the puck to him.

If the situation doesn't call for forechecking, you still should pick up the attacking team as soon as possible. Your wingmen will pick up their wingmen and more or less escort them up the ice. If the wingmen are well covered, then the defensemen should stand up and meet the attacking team at the blueline, or perhaps just in front of it so they can force the puckcarrier to change his direction and throw the play outside (see Figure 29).

But the defense can wait at the blueline only if their wingmen already have picked up the rival wings. If the attacking wingmen are open and the centerman is carrying the puck, then the defense is forced to back up farther into its own end (see Figure 30).

Once the attacking team has penetrated, the defensemen must cover up in front of their net. To defend their goaltender properly, they must not allow anyone to encroach upon that dangerous territory.

At times, one or both defensemen will find themselves outnumbered. We have discussed in further detail earlier what they should do when their team is short-handed, but for now we will consider only the sudden breakaway that occurs when both sides are at equal strength.

The important things for a defenseman to keep in mind at such a time is to play the puck, try to stall for time, and try to force the shot, if there is going to be one, from the side and not from in front of the net.

If you can force the attackers to play with the puck—make an extra pass

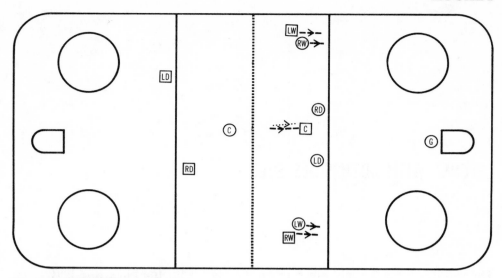

□ = OFFENSIVE PLAYER
○ = DEFENSIVE PLAYER
---- = PATH OF OFFENSIVE PLAYER
—— = PATH OF DEFENSIVE PLAYER
·········· = PATH OF PUCK

Figure 29. Defensive right defenseman and defensive left defenseman stand at blueline as defensive right wing and defensive left wing have offensive left wing and offensive right wing covered.

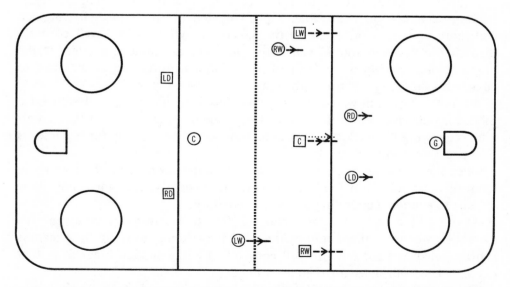

Figure 30. Defensive right defenseman and defensive left defenseman back up across their own blueline as offensive left wing and offensive right wing are not checked. Defensive right defenseman and defensive left defenseman are outnumbered.

or pause to look for an opening—that's all well and good. Your own team-mates are skating back as quickly as they can, and all they need are a few seconds to get back into the play and equalize matters.

Don't let anyone get a shot from the slot, right in front of the goal, and don't let anyone just walk in with the puck. If they must take a shot, let it be from the side, where the goaltender will have a better chance of stopping it.

BREAKAWAYS

The continuous up-and-down flow of hockey provides its own frustrations when you are unable to capitalize on your many forays into enemy ice. But hockey is an opportunistic sport, and you must be alert at all times to take advantage of a sudden break.

You never know when the opportunity will present itself, when you'll suddenly find yourself with the puck and a clear field in front of you.

A bad pass by the other team, a snap interception, an alert deflection by one of your defensemen, a crisp clearing pass from your goaltender after a save—there are many ways the situation can open. To make it work for you, your reaction, and that of your affected teammates, must be instantaneous.

Size up the situation in a flash. The opposition had been on offense, perhaps pressing a strong attack, and some of its members don't even realize yet that they've lost the puck and must get back on defense. Can you mount a three-on-two break, or a two-on-one break, or a one-on-one break? Even while asking this question, you and your teammates should be moving into positions so that if the situation is right, you can take advantage of it before the other team has a chance to react.

Another factor that can be an aid in your breakaway is the bad habit many skaters have of taking a big circle when they want to turn around. For some of them it's just too much work to put the brakes on, stop, and come on back. Instead, they waste precious seconds taking a big turn, giving you those extra moments in which to get your attack going.

The three-on-two or two-on-one breakaway is different from a power play, when one team has a man advantage for a full two minutes. During a power play, you are wise to invest a few seconds while everyone gets into proper position so you can start your attack as a cohesive unit. But there is no such luxury when a sudden turnover, while both sides are even, gives you a breakaway. This can work to your advantage only as long as you are able to keep ahead of the defense, so there is no time to be spared.

This is not to say that you should panic and fluff the opportunity in your haste to get off a shot, but there should be no wasted motion in taking advan-

tage of the break and setting up a suitable scoring chance. You must formu-
late your play even while rushing up ice, keeping in mind that it will take
only a few seconds of grace before the defensive team can regroup and skate
back into the play.

Generally, the same principles can be applied for two-on-one breaks as for
three-on-two breaks. The secret to making the break work is quick reaction
and passing. This doesn't mean merely accurate passing, but also timely passing. It is critical to make your passes at the correct times, and I shall explain
this further as we delve into the subject. Suffice it to say for now that the biggest mistake is to wait too long to make the pass, thus taking the edge off the
break.

A number of the plays applicable to a three-on-two breakaway also apply
to the two-on-one, taking into consideration, of course, the obvious difference
in manpower. First, though, let's consider the two-on-one.

The ideal situation is for the puckcarrier to pull the lone defenseman off to
a side, away from in front of the net, and then pass the puck back to his teammate who has taken the occasion to station himself in front of the net (see
Figure 31). Carried off perfectly, the fellow with the puck now has a head-on
shot from directly in front.

However, it isn't too often in such a situation that you'll succeed in drawing
the defenseman so far out of position. If he does maintain himself in a line in

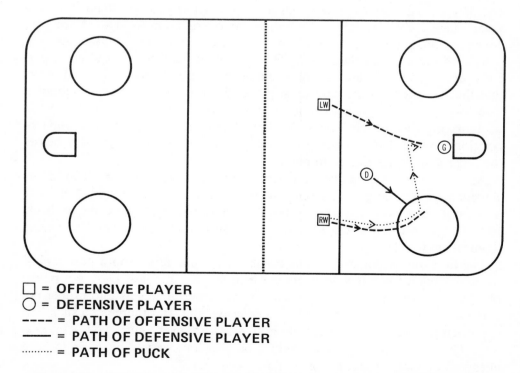

☐ = OFFENSIVE PLAYER
◯ = DEFENSIVE PLAYER
---- = PATH OF OFFENSIVE PLAYER
—— = PATH OF DEFENSIVE PLAYER
········ = PATH OF PUCK

*Figure 31. Offensive right wing pulls defenseman away from middle of ice
and then passes to offensive left wing in front of net.*

front of the net, you'll still be able to draw him slightly off to one side, and reversing himself to come toward you, when you try to cut around him.

Looking at this play from another angle, I'll try to diagram with words the proper method: As you're skating in toward the goal, the defenseman is back-tracking, trying to keep himself as the apex of a triangle between the two players. You suddenly cut either left or right, depending whether you're a left wing or a right wing, in an effort to get around the defenseman. He can't back up fast enough any more, and he reverses himself to skate forward to keep up with you.

At this precise moment, if you have been watching the defenseman closely and spot him reversing from backskating to forward, assuming that you're too deep to get off a good shot, pass the puck quickly to your teammate. A good pass should set up a high-potential shot.

Keep in mind that a defenseman would prefer to remain where he is, in front of his net and facing both attackers. But when you've driven him virtu-ally to the front door of the net and make a move to cut around the de-fenseman, you've succeeded in making him turn his back on your teammate and put him at a great disadvantage.

Another method of coming down two-on-one, instead of one player carry-ing the puck in by himself, is with a series of rapid passes (see Figure 32).

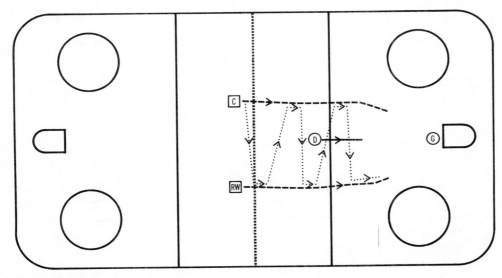

☐ = OFFENSIVE PLAYER
◯ = DEFENSIVE PLAYER
---- = PATH OF OFFENSIVE PLAYER
—— = PATH OF DEFENSIVE PLAYER
········ = PATH OF PUCK

Figure 32. Two-on-one break: Four or five rapid passes are made between offensive center and offensive right wing as they approach defenseman. Defenseman doesn't get time to set himself for one particular pattern as the play is continuously and rapidly changing in front of him.

Make two or three quick passes to each other, and each pass forces the defenseman to change his tactics and to focus his attention on a different player. The key to making this work is to put the puck on your teammate's stick so he doesn't lose a step or juggle it.

The defenseman is unable to settle into any kind of pattern and cannot guess which player will try to cut around him or take a shot.

There is no set standard of how close to each other the two attacking players should be. Ideally, they should be close enough so that their rapid passes will be both crisp and accurate, yet far enough apart so that the defenseman can't get to them both. I'd think that about twenty-five feet (which is roughly one third the width of the rink) would be suitable to serve both purposes.

When a line is coming down on a three-on-two break, it is best if the centerman carries the puck and initiates the play. If he has the time, and wishes to disorient the defense somewhat, the centerman can make an early pass to one of his wings and then receive a return pass (see Figure 33).

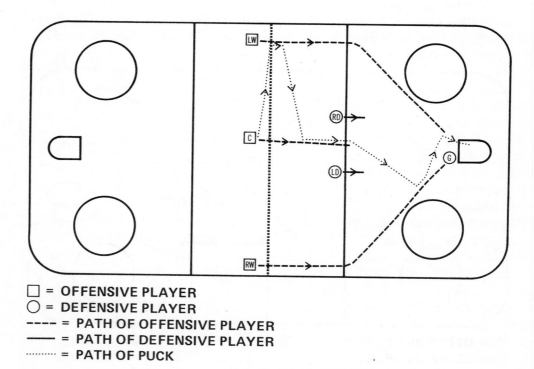

☐ = OFFENSIVE PLAYER
◯ = DEFENSIVE PLAYER
---- = PATH OF OFFENSIVE PLAYER
—— = PATH OF DEFENSIVE PLAYER
········· = PATH OF PUCK

Figure 33.   Three-on-two break: Offensive center passes to offensive left wing at center ice, who returns pass to offensive center just before blueline. Offensive center carries puck across blueline as defensive right defenseman and defensive left defenseman back up. Once puck is over blueline, offensive right wing skates hard for net—bursting behind defensive left defenseman. Offensive center passes puck to offensive right wing, who skates in on goalie. Goalie plays offensive right wing, so offensive right wing passes to offensive left wing, who shoots into open net.

A wingman also can set up the play by carrying the puck or by taking a quick pass from his centerman, and there are several alternatives for either of them to work a man free for a clear shot.

But before a play can be set up in enemy ice, the first big objective is to carry the puck over the blueline with everyone moving and everyone onside. If the centerman is carrying the puck at his redline and one of his wingmen is approaching the blueline, he should throw the puck to the forward man. If the centerman doesn't pass, the wingman is forced to stop, and the defense won't have to worry too much about him, since he's not moving anywhere and has lost his momentum. In this situation, the only alternative for the wingman is to cut parallel along the blueline. If the wingman gets the puck on the move, he'll draw the defense farther back, and he can always drop the puck off for the centerman when that player gets across the blueline.

By the same token, a centerman, or anyone carrying the puck, should be careful not to make a sudden sashay just as he's reaching the blueline. This can throw the play offside, or nullify the breakaway, if his linemates are also caught unaware and continue across the blueline before the puck. Save the fancy steps for after you cross the blueline and the play is safely onside.

If a wingman is the one carrying the puck over the blueline, his immediate objective is to cut around the defenseman guarding him while his centerman remains back in the slot. As with the principle of the two-on-one that we discussed earlier, the wingman tries to get the defenseman to turn with him. At the moment the defenseman does make a move, the wingman, who has been watching him closely out of a corner of his eye, quickly sends the puck back to his centerman (see figure 34).

What the wingman has done is to force the defenseman to commit himself, to turn himself away from the centerman. However, if that wingman doesn't get his pass away at just the right moment, when the defenseman is in the process of turning, then the defenseman will be in position to stop the pass with his stick or his feet.

As I said before, the defenseman would much prefer to face the play, and once he's forced to turn his back on it he's at a big disadvantage.

What, then, does the wingman do if the defenseman doesn't turn with him? Simple. He has an unopposed path to the net, and he can just walk in alone and challenge the goaltender (see Figure 35).

This is the principle of a breakaway. When you have the other team at a disadvantage in manpower, you call the shots. There is no way one defenseman can adequately cover two attacking forwards if they know their business and keep themselves an adequate distance apart. The important thing is to go in driving and force the defenseman to commit himself. If you just coast in with the idea of maintaining your poise and setting up a *perfect* play, the defenseman will be able to float back, always facing the play, knowing that when you eventually make your pass back to the slot, he'll be able to break it up.

Returning to our play with one wingman busting in toward the net and the centerman positioning himself in the slot, the wingman on the far side also should be cutting for the net, trying to pull the second defenseman with him.

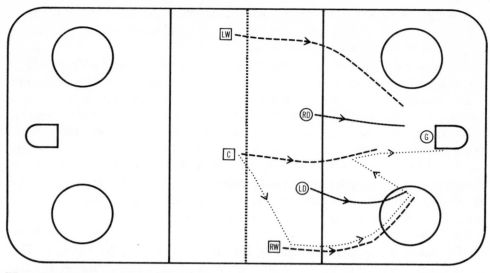

□ = OFFENSIVE PLAYER
○ = DEFENSIVE PLAYER
---- = PATH OF OFFENSIVE PLAYER
—— = PATH OF DEFENSIVE PLAYER
········· = PATH OF PUCK

Figure 34.   Three-on-two break: Offensive center passes to offensive right wing just before blueline, and offensive right wing tries to break around defensive left defenseman. Seeing that defensive left defenseman is going to catch him, offensive right wing passes puck back to offensive center who is in slot, and offensive center shoots and scores. Defensive right defenseman has been busy covering offensive left wing who was bursting in from the left side.

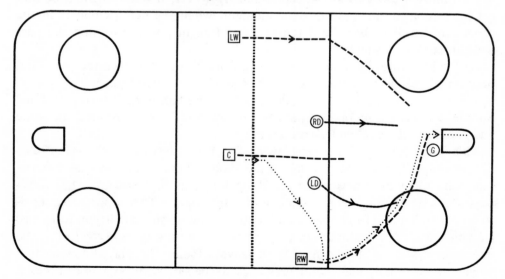

Figure 35.   Three-on-two break: Offensive center passes puck to offensive right wing just before latter's feet cross blueline, and offensive right wing, skating at full speed, is able to break around defensive left defenseman and go in and score.

If that wingman doesn't cut, the second defenseman is able to stay out and cover both him and the centerman. By cutting, the wingman takes the pressure off the centerman and also puts himself in position to receive a pass in front of the net, deflect a shot by one of his teammates, or pick up a rebound.

Thus, as we have seen, the wingman carrying the puck has three plays: He can take the shot himself if he has beaten the defenseman; he can pass back to the centerman, making the pass at the moment the defenseman turns to meet him; or he can send the puck across to the front of the net to the far-side wingman who has busted through.

If everyone has done his job right, it is inevitable that someone gets a good, clear shot. The wingman carrying the puck has the shot if he gets around the first defenseman; the centerman has it if the two defensemen cover the two breaking wingmen; and the far-side wingman has it if the second defenseman neglects him to cover the center spot.

The centerman carrying the puck on a breakaway also has his choices, and a smart player will predicate his own moves on the type of defense that greets him.

Once over the blueline, if he isn't being chased and has the time, the centerman can put on the brakes in hopes of preventing the defense from pulling back deeper into its own zone. Should the defense hesitate, the centerman then whips a pass to one of his breaking wingmen who possibly can cut in behind the stalled defense.

However, if the defense continues backing in toward its own goal, the centerman can skate in and take the shot himself, timing it, if possible, to reach the net just as his wingmen are barreling through (see Figure 36). This flurry

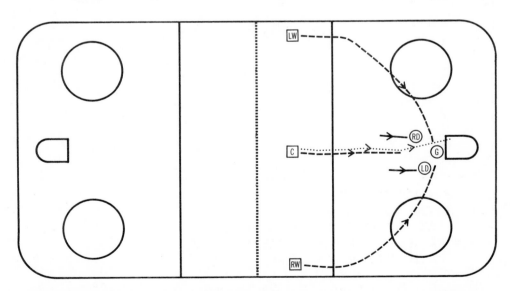

Figure 36. Three-on-two break: Offensive center carries puck over blueline, and defensive right defenseman and defensive left defenseman back in on top of their goalie. Offensive left wing and offensive right wing skate for front of goal. Offensive center keeps puck and skates straight for goalie, shooting just as offensive left wing and offensive right wing reach front of goal.

of action can certainly confuse the goaltender, not to mention the fact that he quite possibly can be screened on the shot, and again the wingmen are in position for a deflection or a rebound.

Another alternative on the three-on-two is for the centerman to pass to his right wingman (or left wingman, as the case may be) just as they cross the blueline, then bust between the defensemen straight for the net. The right wingman then returns the puck to the centerman, while in the meantime the left wingman, instead of breaking for the net himself, skates over into the slot vacated by the centerman (see Figure 37).

What is happening, in effect, is that the centerman has drawn the second defenseman to him because of his rush, leaving the left wingman unguarded in the slot. If they get the puck to him, he has the open shot (see Figure 38). If the second defenseman didn't pull with the centerman, then he's the one in the clear for an open shot.

For those who like to live dangerously, this next play is for you. The centerman carries the puck over the blueline and has one wingman busting for the net and the other moving behind him. The centerman then drops the puck for this second wingman, who probably is unguarded (see Figure 39).

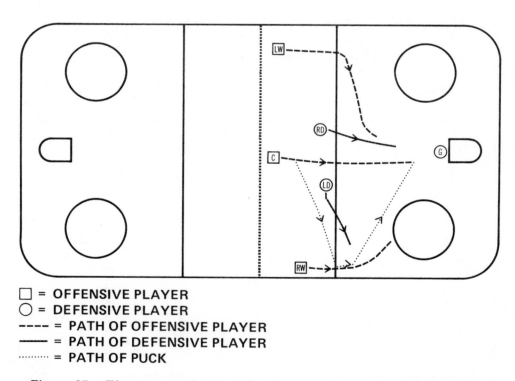

☐ = OFFENSIVE PLAYER
◯ = DEFENSIVE PLAYER
---- = PATH OF OFFENSIVE PLAYER
—— = PATH OF DEFENSIVE PLAYER
·········· = PATH OF PUCK

Figure 37. Three-on-two break: Offensive center passes to offensive right wing at blueline, and offensive center breaks between defensive right defenseman and defensive left defenseman and receives return pass from offensive right wing. In the meantime, offensive left wing cuts into slot for possible pass and also as safety valve. Offensive center gets shot on goal.

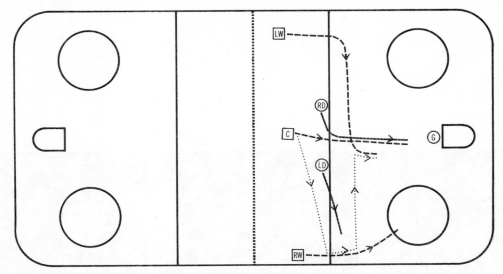

Figure 38. Three-on-two break: Offensive center passes to offensive right wing at blueline, and offensive center breaks between defensive left defenseman and defensive right defenseman. Defensive right defenseman stays right with offensive center. In the meantime, offensive left wing, who cut into slot, receives pass from offensive right wing and has good scoring opportunity.

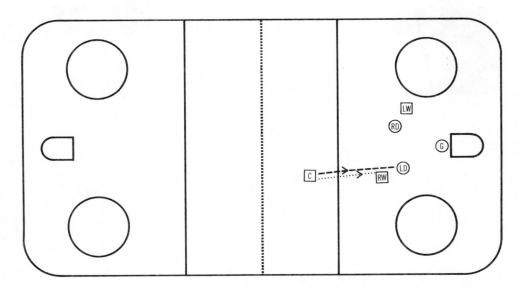

Figure 39.   Drop pass: Offensive center carries puck over blueline and skates straight at defensive left defenseman, dropping puck to offensive right wing who is directly behind offensive center just before meeting defensive left defenseman. Offensive center acts as a shield, blocking out defensive left defenseman so that offensive right wing can get a good screened shot, can carry puck right in on goal, or can pass to offensive left wing if he is open.

This can be a dangerous play because if you make a bad drop, or the wingman isn't in the exact spot where you left the puck, the play may come to an untimely end and all three of you will be caught going the wrong way while the opposition suddenly springs a breakaway on you.

In hockey, one has to keep in mind that it's not always what you do so much as what you leave the other team. Don't gamble to such an extent that you get yourself trapped up ice and leave yourself with a weak flank. It is easy to give up a goal in hockey, but far more difficult to score one.

Get the puck moving toward the enemy net as fast as possible. Regardless of what level of hockey you're playing, from the first grade to the National Hockey League, it is important that you do things in a hurry. When you dillydally on a breakaway, you're simply giving away your advantage, since the players on the other team who were trapped up ice are steaming back into the play as quickly as possible.

The quicker you make your play, the more chance it will stand of success and the better you will become at making it. As you move into the higher levels of competition, speed of mind and body becomes more and more essential.

DEFENSING THE BREAKAWAY

When a defenseman finds himself on the short side of a breakaway, whether it be two-on-one or three-on-two for the other team, his immediate concern is to prevent the attacking forwards from working their way around him and setting up a direct confrontation with the goaltender. The best way to defeat this is to back up a little farther than usual, all the time maintaining a vigilant guard against being faked out of the play.

When you're outnumbered it is also imperative to play the puck, not the man, and to stall for time where possible so that your forwards can come back and perhaps negate the breakaway before any real damage is done. The way to stall is to let the opposition move as slowly as it wants to. Don't force them into making quick moves as a means of getting by you, and where possible try to induce them to make the final play to the back man, since he is the one who can be caught most quickly by the backcheckers.

If you are alone defending against two attackers, the ideal position as you skate backward is to remain near the center of the ice at a point equally between them (see Figure 40). In effect, you are the point of a triangle. Do not allow yourself to be pulled off to one side of the net unless you know you will be able to sprawl out at the key moment and block a cross-ice pass or a shot. This is a risky gamble and is best left to the experienced and capable player.

But whether you be a novice peewee or a battle-scarred forty-year-old veteran, it helps immeasurably if you have done your homework and have a "book" on your rivals. Who is the better scorer of the two men attacking? Is one more likely to pass or to shoot the puck himself? Are you matched against a fancy skater, one who is capable of the quick move that can carry him around you?

When you are familiar with your competition and are able to react spontaneously to the situation, it is very much in your power to outwit the attackers and force them to make the play you want them to. For example, you might make a sudden move toward the puckcarrier, not really intending to go at him, but with the knowledge of past experience that once you make a move, he's going to throw the puck to his teammate. This puts you in position to in-

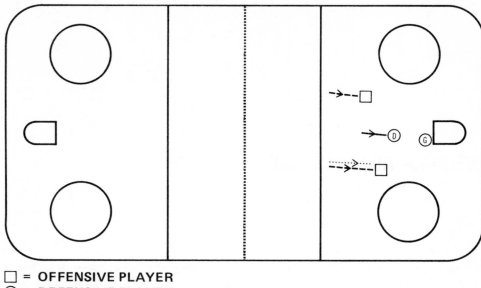

☐ = OFFENSIVE PLAYER
◯ = DEFENSIVE PLAYER
---- = PATH OF OFFENSIVE PLAYER
—— = PATH OF DEFENSIVE PLAYER
········ = PATH OF PUCK

Figure 40. Defenseman skates backward facing the two attackers and backs in farther than he would if it were one-on-one, making sure he doesn't get pulled away from in front of the net unless he is sure of getting the puck.

tercept the puck or merely to deflect it, either way breaking up the attack.

Even if the pass does go through, you still have created the situation of dictating which of the forwards will take the shot, and from what angle. You are working in partnership with your goaltender, and if it is apparent that a shot is going to be taken, you want to insure that it won't be a good one, that it is taken by the weaker member of the attackers and from as bad an angle as possible, so that your goaltender will have the best chance of making the save.

If it is at all possible, force your opponent to take his shot from the side, knowing your goaltender will have a much better chance to cut down the angle and block the shot than he would if it was taken from directly in front of the net. Once the puck is on the side, your goaltender should have that short side well covered, and your job then is to make certain that a return pass isn't made to the open side of the net, where the other forward would have an easy shot.

Your reactions should be basically the same if you're defending against a three-on-two break. You and your partner station yourselves toward the middle of the ice as you backpedal so that you're in position to float one way or another, depending on what the forwards do (see Figure 41). You must be prepared to react to their actions.

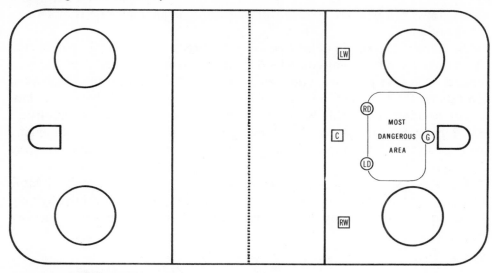

☐ = OFFENSIVE PLAYER
○ = DEFENSIVE PLAYER
---- = PATH OF OFFENSIVE PLAYER
—— = PATH OF DEFENSIVE PLAYER
········· = PATH OF PUCK

Figure 41. Three-on-two break: Defensive right defenseman and defensive left defenseman should back in a little farther than normal and should not let themselves get pulled away from the goal unless they're sure of blocking or getting control of the puck. The best place to score is from in front of the goal. The ruled zone shows the area that is most dangerous; normally, defensive left defenseman and defensive right defenseman should try not to be pulled away from that area.

A wingman carrying the puck into your zone on a breakaway has three basic options: He can walk in on the net himself if you give him enough room; he can pass back to the centerman, who usually stays in the slot; or he can throw it straight across in front of the net to the other wingman coming down the opposite lane.

The defenseman playing the puckcarrier can't let him cut around him, and if you see that the winger is trying to pass or shoot, your job is to get a piece of his stick or arm or anything that will throw him off balance even slightly. He may get a shot away, but it won't be as dangerous a shot.

The other defenseman, meantime, must size up the situation and try to prevent the puck from getting through to either the other winger or centerman and to prevent them from cutting in toward the goal.

After you've played together with another defenseman for a number of games, you are each aware of what the other will do and of individual responsibilities in given situations. It's like your right hand and your left hand. If something slips from your right hand, you catch it with your left. It's the same with defensemen who are used to working with one another; one compensates for the other.

Once again, the key in defending against a break is to maintain correct position until the offense has committed itself. If a wingman cuts wide and puts himself deep into a corner, don't follow him. Just leave him there and concentrate on the two men in front until such time as he moves back into dangerous position. If he simply shoots from that corner, you've accomplished your job, because the goaltender, working along with you, should be hugging the post and have the angle cut off perfectly so that he will be able to make the stop.

If you've lost your man—and this is very important—don't make a futile attempt to catch him if you know you can't. Instead, once he's skated by you, move quickly to cover any of his teammates who are open and in dangerous position.

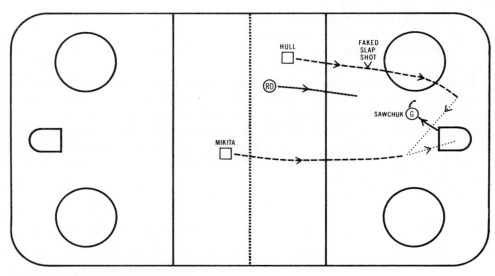

☐ = OFFENSIVE PLAYER
◯ = DEFENSIVE PLAYER
---- = PATH OF OFFENSIVE PLAYER
—— = PATH OF DEFENSIVE PLAYER
········ = PATH OF PUCK

Figure 42. Hull had defensive right defenseman beaten and went to slap puck. Goalie Sawchuk moved out of net and cut angle down. Hull saw he couldn't score, so he held puck. However, his speed had now carried him past the goal and he couldn't score, so he passed the puck to Mikita, who was all alone in front of the net, and he scored. The defensive right defenseman was still chasing Hull although he had no chance of catching him. Mikita had skated in late from behind the play and from behind defensive right defenseman. Defensive right defenseman could have checked Mikita, nullifying play.

I can remember one occasion when I was coaching Los Angeles and the late Terry Sawchuk was my goaltender. Bobby Hull broke in on him from the left wing, and although he was at an angle to the goal, he still possessed one of the great booming shots in hockey. Sawchuk came way out of his net to meet Hull and cut down his angle and just bundled himself into a tight ball, steeling himself for the shot.

Hull instinctively saw that no matter how hard he shot, there was no way he was going to get the puck into the net unless he blasted right through Sawchuk. So he quickly changed his tactics and took the puck deeper into the corner, from where he couldn't score, then passed to a teammate right in front of the net, Stan Mikita, who had a wide-open net into which to shoot (see Figure 42).

The crowd in Los Angeles thought Sawchuk had made a real goof on the play, but of course the goof was made by Terry's teammates. The defensemen, who were beaten on the play, didn't pick up the open man. They couldn't catch Hull anyway, so they should have picked up the man Hull could have passed to. If they had done that, Chicago never would have scored a goal on the play because Sawchuk had Hull beaten. Our players, who for the most part were new to the league, weren't aware of this, and they learned a good lesson.

DEFENSEMEN

Anytime both teams are at full strength, they generally ice three men whose primary function is offense and three men who are concerned mainly with defense. Ice hockey being what it is, with its constant flow from one end of the rink to the other, it is always everyone's responsibility to help stop the other team from scoring, just as all players, with the possible exception of the goaltender, join efforts on attack.

Defensemen, though, are the ones who feel the finger of guilt pointed at them whenever a goal is allowed, and their function of preventing goals is equally important to the overall success of a team as the ability of their forwards to score goals.

A defenseman is similar to a quarterback in football. He can control the flow of the game better than anyone, breaking up oncoming rushes and then starting the play back the other way. Just as a quarterback determines the success or failure of any play by how he starts it, so does the defenseman in getting the attack organized in his own end. It is vitally important to get the play started right, for if it is started right, there's every chance it's going to end right.

Although his primary job isn't to score, a defenseman must be skilled at handling the puck and passing it. He may have a wingman skating at a speed of twenty miles an hour away from him, yet he must hit him on the fly with the puck to get the play off to a moving start from his own end. Or the defenseman might be chugging along at five or ten miles an hour and one of his teammates is going at close to thirty, and he still must hit him with a crisp, accurate pass.

To do this, the defenseman must develop a keen sense of timing and judgment, and must be able to thread a hole between moving skates in order to hit a teammate. A slow or off-target pass in such situations can be suicide for the intended receiver, because while he's looking for it, some other guy will bodycheck him into the fifth row. Appropriately enough, we call this a suicide pass.

More so than a forward, who need only be swift, shifty, and elusive when he's skating ahead, a defenseman must be just as mobile skating backward as he is forward, and he must be able to turn either way without losing a stride. These are standard skills for a rear guard in any league, and more essential than any bulk or size he may have.

Remember, a defenseman continually is called upon to skate backward toward his own goal, and at the same time he must prevent a rival who is skating forward from getting around him, be prepared to shift his attention to someone else if a pass is made, keep in mind how close he is drawing to his own net and his goaltender although they are behind him, and be ready to initiate an offensive attack should his team suddenly get the puck.

Basically, a defenseman should remain firm on both feet at all times so that he's able to twist either to the left or the right when he's backpedaling. When he's defensing a man, he should hold his stick out in front of him as far as possible to gain some extra time in reacting to a move, as well as possibly breaking up the play with the stick.

If you, as a defenseman, keep your stick at your feet or off to a side, then the attacking player can step right up to your nose before making his move, giving you absolutely no time in which to react. However, if you hold your stick at arm's length ahead of you, this forces the attacker to stay some six feet away from you and give you that extra time in which to counter his move.

Balance is the key, and a lot of this comes with experience. If you swing your stick too much from side to side, you'll throw yourself off balance. Just sit back there, secure on both feet, and make little arm movements with your stick. Hopefully, you may be able to poke the puck away, but even if you don't, you are still leaving yourself with a good chance to break up the play by holding the stick far in front of you.

When backing in, a defenseman should take care not to move too close to his goaltender. He also must try not to accidentally deflect a shot so that it changes direction and catches the goaltender going the wrong way, and he should try not to screen his goaltender from the play.

The goaltender likes to see the puck, to follow the shot as it approaches him. The defenseman can help him by not getting in his way, by not allowing the shooter to move in too close, and by forcing the shot, if possible, from an angle rather than from directly in front of the net.

The defensemen and the goaltender must work together if they are to have any hope of stopping the opposition. It is up to the individuals involved to decide beforehand how they will react to various situations, and then they must practice over and over again the different plays so that there won't be a moment lost due to hesitation during the heat of real battle.

Often, if a shot is coming from an angle and the goaltender is slightly screened by his own defenseman or a rival player, he will let the defenseman —if he is an adept puck blocker—play the short side, since he is closer to the action. In the meantime, the goaltender will watch carefully the far side of the net in the event of a shot by the puckcarrier to the far side or a quick pass. Or it can be done the other way, with the goaltender always covering the short side of the cage and the defenseman guarding the far side.

In planning your strategy, it should be considered how good a shot blocker each particular defenseman is, and this of course influences the manner in which you will handle various situations.

The defenseman who is guarding against a breakaway should remember to maintain his position in relation to his net and not be pulled too far off to the side. One of the two forwards on a two-on-one break may skate into a corner, hoping to pull the defenseman to him. If the defenseman falls for this trap, then the wingman will simply toss the puck to his teammate, who is by now open in front of the net.

If the forward takes the puck into the corner, let him go. It isn't likely that he's going to score from there. Then, if the forward realizes he's not going to trap the defenseman, he may skate in from the side toward the goal. The goaltender should have that short side pretty well covered up, and the defenseman prevents the puckcarrier from going beyond the short side of the net, from where he might have an open net to shoot into. Of course, if the puckcarrier is in the corner and passes to his teammate near the net, the defenseman, who hasn't been lured out of position, is ready to guard that man. But all the time that the offensive team is setting up its shot, other members of the defensive unit are skating back and are soon ready to join the play.

This is just one of many examples of a defenseman's duties in conjunction with his goaltender, and two entire chapters in this book are devoted to breakaways and the defensing of them.

Placing the defenseman in his most simple perspective, it is his duty to stay between the puckcarrier and the goal. If he can always remember that, he can avoid a lot of problems.

An offensive player is always trying to pull the defenseman away from in front of the net so that he can go in and have a head-on open shot, or pass to a teammate who will be in the clear. Beware of tricky stickhandlers. They may make a motion of moving the puck to one side or the other, then, if the defenseman falls for the bait and leans toward that side, they can pull the puck right back and be home free.

There is one golden rule a defenseman should always bear in mind when he is under attack: "If I stay between you and the net, then you're defeated."

This may seem such a simple concept, yet defensemen keep making the same mistake of forgetting it all the way up to and in the National Hockey League. One of my men at Pittsburgh once cost us a goal when a forward faked him out of position by throwing the puck over to one side, then quickly retrieving it. If my defenseman had played the man instead of the puck, the forward wouldn't have been able to go around him and wouldn't have had the shot.

A defenseman should play the man, since it is the man who eventually will have to shoot the puck at the goal, *but* the defenseman should be aware where the puck is at all times. You can't just forget the puck entirely to concentrate solely on the man.

There is an excellent drill that you can use to help develop your peripheral vision, and this ability is essential to anyone who wants to play the game, regardless of his position. It is a simple drill where a player stands still with one arm stretched high and the other hanging low. He then concentrates on focusing his eyes so that both hands are within his view without having to move his head. At first the hands needn't be stretched too far apart, with the distance between them increasing as the person's peripheral vision improves.

It is just as important, of course, for a player to be able to see on both sides of him without having to turn his head constantly, and the arm exercise is effective in developing this ability. Here, the arms are stretched wide apart, rather than up and down, and objects placed on either side of a person, perhaps even scattered in various places, can be used.

The puckcarrier doesn't look down at the puck when he's moving it along the ice, and neither can the defenseman afford to keep his eyes down. The defenseman should be able to see the puck while playing an opponent eyeball to eyeball. In addition, the defenseman must know where every other player on the ice is. This is important for any player, but particularly for a defenseman. If he sees four rival players, he'd better find out quickly where the fifth man is, because that's the guy who will get him.

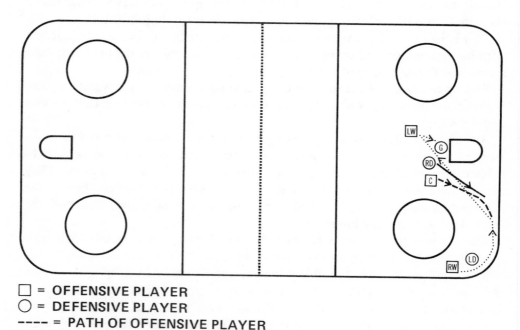

☐ = OFFENSIVE PLAYER
◯ = DEFENSIVE PLAYER
---- = PATH OF OFFENSIVE PLAYER
—— = PATH OF DEFENSIVE PLAYER
········· = PATH OF PUCK

Figure 43. Defensive left defenseman is in corner trying to check offensive right wing. Defensive right defenseman is covering front of goal. Offensive center, who is in front of goal, skates to boards at side of net to pick up puck, which offensive right wing poked loose. Defensive right defenseman follows offensive center, who retrieves loose puck and centers to offensive left wing, who is all alone in front of goal. Both defensive left defenseman and defensive right defenseman are caught away from the front of goal.

One of the more common failings of defensemen in this regard is when they get hypnotized by a player who's behind the net or near the side of it with the puck. This man must be watched, but in doing so, some defensemen have a tendency to turn their backs on and ignore another player who is in front of the net. The player standing in front of the net is the most dangerous person in the rink, and the defensemen must be alert to any rival who is in that position.

When a team is under attack, at least one of its defensemen should maintain a permanent position in front of his net (see Figure 43). If he is defending against a particular player, and that player decides to skate behind the net, for example, the defenseman remains in his original position. The other defenseman can follow the play behind the net, or into a corner, if the situation calls for it. An exception to this rule is when he knows he can get the puck.

The net, incidentally, is a very powerful weapon for the player who knows how to use it, and it makes an effective shield. If a defenseman has the puck and someone is chasing him, he can cut that player off at the net and gain the necessary time to start the play moving the other way (see Figure 44 right). If a defenseman doesn't use the net properly, he allows the opposition to check him into the boards and take him out of the play (see Figure 44

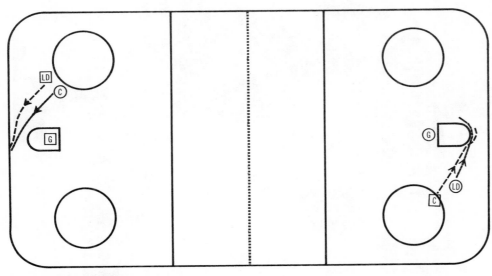

□ = OFFENSIVE PLAYER
○ = DEFENSIVE PLAYER
---- = PATH OF OFFENSIVE PLAYER
—— = PATH OF DEFENSIVE PLAYER
·········· = PATH OF PUCK

Figure 44. At right, defensive left defenseman used net to cut off checker, offensive center, and was able to carry puck out. At left, offensive left defenseman failed to use net and checker, defensive center, was able to ride offensive left defenseman into boards and get puck.

left). But by cutting close to the net, the defenseman forces his pursuer to either run into the net or to take the longer outside route around him. This is similar to racehorses fighting for the rail position on a turn.

Defensemen and forwards alike can use the net and the goaltender as a shield behind which to change gears. Let's say you're cutting around the back of the net with the puck and a rival player is moving toward the front of the net to check you. He sees the speed at which you're skating, and he times his own movement to set up a collision course. But at the split second that the net and the goaltender shield you from his view, you can shift into a faster gear and be past him with that extra stride or two. When shifting gears, it should be done with no visible sign in your skating motion.

The defenseman now has the puck in the open, and it is up to him to get his own team's attack off to an effective start. I spoke of this at the beginning of the chapter, and I'd like to conclude by returning to the defenseman's role on offense.

As I said earlier, the defenseman is the quarterback of the team, the man who controls the game more than anyone else. He breaks up attacks directed at his team, and then initiates the action going the other way. The quicker he is able to get the puck moving up ice following the turnover, the more off balance he'll catch the other team and the better chance he'll have of putting his team on the scoreboard.

With all due credit to Bobby Orr and others like him, this seems to be the age of the rushing defenseman. Yet we can't all move like Orr, and so we must understand when it is wise to rush and wiser yet to pass off quickly to a forward.

The time to rush is when you've caught the opposition short-handed. If you've suddenly taken the puck away from the other team and they don't have time to react to the change, this is ample reason for the defenseman to carry the puck. He'll probably be joined by one of his forwards who had been slowed down by his backchecking chores, and together they can mount a break.

However, if all the members of the other team are in front of him and ready, it's far better for the defenseman to allow his forwards to carry the puck. This allows the defenseman to trail the play and be ready to handle the situation should the other team suddenly take the puck away, and also to conserve his strength for a better opportunity to rush the puck.

When the defenseman does make a rush, he should still keep in mind who he is. He can make his thrust into enemy territory, but rather than hanging around there in hopes of another chance, he must wheel back to his defensive position. In the meantime, while he is in the process of making his initial drive, a teammate should be covering up for him.

GOALTENDERS

Talk about a man on a spot, there can't be anyone in any sport who is under more pressure, both physical and mental, than a goaltender. He is the single person focused on and under attack from every skater on the opposing team. A goaltender isn't allowed a mistake. Each mistake can mean a goal, and each goal in hockey can be priceless. The goaltender is the last line of defense, and he doesn't have anyone waiting behind him to cover up his mistakes.

It's an oddity of the game that many goaltenders got their first indoctrination behind the mask because they may have been the slowest skater in the crowd when they were growing up. Yet a goaltender must be strong physically to stand up to the constant sieges on his person and the net, and strong mentally to cope with the extraordinary pressures of the job.

Much of the job of goaltending is instinct. Constant practice is the only way to develop that instinct, but there are some basics that every goaltender should keep in mind.

The first basic of goaltending is to remain on your feet. It's a natural tendency for a goaltender to fall to the ice in anticipation of a shot, but once he's off his feet, he's at the mercy of the shooter. He sacrifices his mobility and is defenseless against a high shot. And even if he does make a save by falling to the ice, he is out of the picture in the event of a rebound.

It is even more important for a smaller goaltender to stay on his feet than it is for a bigger fellow. Lack of height is no real barrier to a player hoping to make the National Hockey League as a goaltender, but this is one of the fatal pitfalls he must be wary of. Once you're off your feet and on the ice, you're conceding a lot of room to the top portion of your net, and you can be certain the opposition will take advantage of it.

If you remain on your feet, though, it is relatively a lot easier to move to your right or left in pursuit of a rebound. I say "relatively" because it is never easy to contend with a snap second or third shot after handling the initial shot. But more on that a little later.

A big goaltender, and Ken Dryden is an excellent example of this type, can afford to go down on his knees because his arm reach is still long enough to protect the upper portions of the net. Some taller goaltenders go down in a spread-eagle fashion with their toes pointed out toward the corners. They go down with their knees inward in such a position that they can rise again in an instant. Even they don't flop to the ice haphazardly, but they maintain control of their body so they can react instantly to a changing situation and change direction themselves.

Briefly, a goaltender should stay on his feet as long as he can. It is much harder to score on a goaltender who maintains his balance than one who is prone to fall to the ice. If a goaltender must go down, he should do so in a way that enables him to remain mobile.

Goaltenders should not be scored upon on the short side—that is, the side they are protecting from an attacking skater. If the wingman is charging down his left lane, then the goaltender should stand up tight against the goal post on the right, or short, side. If a goaltender is beaten on the short side, he is beating himself (see Figure 45).

A defenseman working with his goaltender will try to force an oncoming forward to the outside so that if he gets a shot, the angle will be a bad one. And if the goaltender freezes that short side, virtually hangs onto the short-side post, the forward won't have much of an opening at which to aim. If the

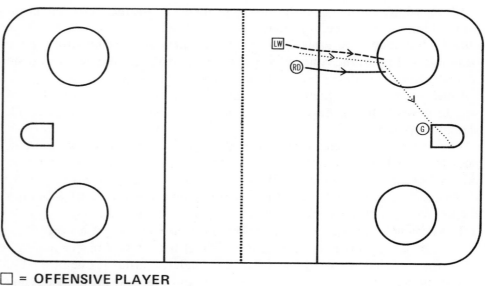

□ = OFFENSIVE PLAYER
○ = DEFENSIVE PLAYER
---- = PATH OF OFFENSIVE PLAYER
—— = PATH OF DEFENSIVE PLAYER
········ = PATH OF PUCK

Figure 45. Goalie failed to protect short side, and offensive left wing scored from bad angle even though he was being checked by defensive right defense-man and could not have cut to goal in order to score on far side of net.

shooter has to aim for the far side, there is more of a chance that the defenseman or some other player will be able to deflect the shot, and since the puck has to travel a greater distance, the goaltender also will have an extra moment in which to react.

A goaltender should know how to use his stick and handle the puck. The stick is invaluable in preventing goals, and is almost as important offensively if the goaltender can help himself by being able to feed a teammate. By starting the play going the other way, the goaltender naturally relieves himself for the moment of the pressure from attack.

Just as relevant is knowing when *not* to use the stick or handle the puck. The puck may be sitting within reach of the goaltender, but at the same time his defenseman may be chasing back after the puck with an opposing player hot on his tail. In this position it is foolish for the goaltender to try to help his teammate by poking the puck toward him, because just that little poke as the defenseman is moving on top of the puck could cause him to overskate it and miss it completely.

I've seen this happen many times, the defenseman skating back at full speed only to have the position of the puck moved at the last moment, and he goes right past it. The opposing player in pursuit, with more time to react to the new position, couldn't ask for a better chance at scoring a goal.

I was mentioning before the danger of rebounds, and there is something the goaltender can do to minimize them. The obvious answer is to catch the puck, and that will put an end to rebounds. Many times, though, it is all a goaltender can do to stop the first shot from going past him.

The most dangerous shot, as far as the goaltender is concerned, is the low one. The goaltender is likely to stop the shot with his skates, the lower extremities of his legs, or his stick, and these parts are unlikely to stop the puck dead so the goaltender can freeze it.

But while he can't control it, the goaltender can learn how to deflect such shots to the corners, away from that dangerous area in front of the net. Developing this skill requires long, long practice sessions, but they are worth every sacrifice because the goaltender who gives rebounds in front of his net is going to be a very sorry one.

It is helpful to have a "book" on the opposition. This is a study of their habits, such as what kind of shots a certain player likes to take, which part of the ice he prefers to shoot from, whether he's likely to fake a shot and then pass, how fast his shot travels, if it tends to stay low or take off, and so on.

Like everything else, this "book" must be used with some reservations in mind. For example, you just can't rely on the memory that the last time you went against a certain player he beat you twice with high shots, and then look only for high shots whenever he takes aim at you. Give the other guy some credit for intelligence and the ability to change his patterns.

But it is to your advantage if you know that a certain individual can only turn effectively to his left when he goes into a corner. You know which way he's going to come out of it if he lacks a degree of maneuverability, and this gives you a jump on him.

There are key aspects of a goaltender's job other than simply stopping pucks. As I indicated before, he should be able to pass to a moving teammate and, particularly when his team is short-handed, it is handy if he can clear the puck. Since the goaltender is facing the play at all times, he should always know what is happening in front of him. He should talk to his teammates and try to direct them, perhaps letting them know where to throw the puck.

It is unfortunate that it is the goaltender who is usually blamed by un-knowledgeable people for lost games. All his mistakes, as well as those that aren't his, shine as bright as a red light. But the rewards are commensurately satisfactory when his team wins.

Generally, it is easy to lay down the proper procedures of good goaltend-ing: Stay on your feet as long as possible, cut down the angle, catch the puck or else deflect it to the side to eliminate the dangers of rebounds, know how to handle your stick, work as a unit with your defensemen, and so on.

But one thing not to be lost sight of, even in peewee hockey, is that a goal-tender remains an individual, and as such has his own individual ways of get-ting the job done. Just as in baseball, where each hitter has his own batting style, so in hockey various goaltenders go about their business in different ways.

When I first broke into hockey, it was accepted style for a goaltender to plant himself in front of his net and stay there. You saw very little wandering. Then along came Jacques Plante, who just couldn't stand still in one place. He had his differences with Toe Blake, then the Canadiens' coach, but Plante thought for himself, and he had the talent to support his ideas.

Early in his career, Plante would get caught a few times far out of his net, but as time went on, and his teammates learned to anticipate his moves, he proved very effective. He'd invariably get caught out of position on odd occa-sions, but he felt he saved far more goals by coming out to meet the opposi-tion, and effectively cutting off the net, than he allowed by being trapped once in a while. His seven Vezina trophies, including five in a row, certainly are testaments to his talent.

Plante, who also was the first modern-day goalie among NHL goaltenders to use a face mask, also helped himself immensely with his ability to handle the puck once he made the stop. Ed Giacomin is another goaltender who is very good with his stick. He'll catch the puck, drop it quickly to his stick, and then pass up ice to one of his forwards, thus trapping an opposing forward or forechecker behind the play. Giacomin set a record by assisting on two goals in a single game in 1972, on both occasions setting up the play by passing to a teammate at mid-ice.

While other goaltenders picked up Plante's style of going out to meet the play, Glenn Hall introduced his own twist by skating out to challenge an on-coming rival and cut off his angle, then falling back toward his net. You have to be very quick to do this, have a precise sense of timing, and be able to judge distance. Hall, of course, had all of these and was a constant source of frustration to rival players, who just didn't know what to expect of him.

Hall also had a great glove hand, and he had an unusual style of sprawling,

with his legs and his feet spread out from goalpost to goalpost. As a result, he had spectacular success in cutting off low corner shots.

Hall, incidentally, put on the best display of a goaltender's staying on his feet that I ever saw. He was playing for St. Louis in a Stanley Cup final game at Boston, and the Bruins fired three point-blank shots at him with almost machine-gun rapidity, but each time Glenn was in position to make the save. Unfortunately, he lost his balance slightly making the third save, and the fourth shot went by him. In almost all cases, though, the three saves he did make should have given his teammates sufficient chance to clear the puck out of danger.

Terry Sawchuk and Johnny Bower were other great stand-up goaltenders with individual characteristics. Sawchuk introduced to hockey what is known as the crouching style. He'd stay on his feet but bend over as low as he could so he could see the pucks coming through the crowd. He felt that on low shots he had a better chance of spotting them low rather than trying to see over the heads of players or around them.

Bower stayed on his feet as long as possible, dropping down only in a crucial situation, and so he was more effective than most in stopping the second, third, or even fourth shots. He was also one of the best in the game at using his stick, and any player who felt he could skate in on Johnny and try to fake around him quite often found himself separated from the puck.

These were great stand-up goaltenders, yet this also is no true criterion in determining what is right and what is wrong. There have been great goaltenders who like to leave their feet, and for examples you need look no farther than Ken Dryden and Tony Esposito.

Dryden, of course, is very big, standing six feet, four inches, and he has a good catching hand. He's also real cool when the action gets frantic, and he's very tough even at close range. Because of his bulk, even when he falls to his knees Dryden is able to protect the upper portions of his net. His quick reflexes and good glove are invaluable aids.

Esposito isn't as big as Dryden, but when he goes down, he keeps his body up, and you don't get much of a view of the top part of the net. He has it well covered with his shoulders. When Tony first came into the league, the word went out among the players that he could be beaten high, and it certainly seemed that that would be the case. Tony has proved them wrong.

One goaltender who had a style that has not been copied since was Bill Durnan. He was a big man, and he was ambidextrous. While a skater was coming in on him, Durnan was able to switch his stick and glove from hand to hand, depending on which side the player was coming down. In this way, Durnan always had his glove hand ready to protect the far, or open, side of the net.

This was a tremendous advantage, since the stick side is considered to be the weaker side of a goaltender. And he too was big enough to get down on his knees and still have enough body left to be above the net. I don't remember ever seeing Durnan get caught with his defenses down while he was switching the stick from one hand to the other.

All these men I've mentioned had their own styles, suited to their individual strengths and capabilities. These styles were developed over years of training and practice as youngsters, and they fit the person who used them like a glove.

Again, this doesn't mean that a player with some natural talent can just throw away the books, ignore his coach, and go his own way. The basic precepts of good goaltending, as outlined in this chapter, remain the same for everyone. It's only when you understand these, and can practice them, that it is safe to experiment with something a little different.

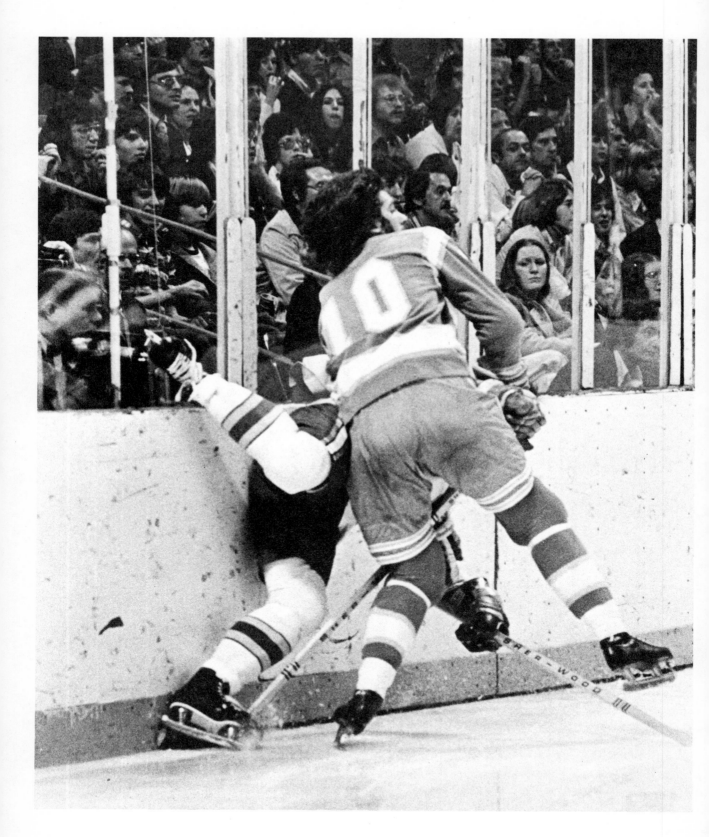

CHECKING

If this book were to carry a subtitle, it might very well be *The Importance of Defense*. And even if it doesn't receive this attention on the cover, defense is the recurring theme that pops up in almost every chapter. Just as multiplication tables and proper grammatical forms are drummed into youngsters at an early age in grade school, so must hockey students be made aware of the place of defense in a winning unit.

To play defense, one must be able to check. Checking is the physical act of preventing your rival from roaming free on the ice, from doing what he wants to do without interference. You can check with your body or with your stick, and checking can play just as important a role in your offensive plans as it is essential in defense.

Tight checking prevents the other team from firing away at your goaltender, and thus prevents them from scoring. Reduced to its most basic level, the ability of a team to check indicates how many times they will have to score in order to win.

A number of teams have gone on to win the Stanley Cup more on their checking ability than their proficiency at scoring goals. This is because a really good checking team can upset the style of an offensive-minded team and at times overcome them. A good example of this was the last Stanley Cup champion I played with when Toronto beat Chicago in six games in 1967. The Hawks were really flying then, with Bobby Hull and Stan Mikita at their best, and they were favored to run over us in the semifinal.

Toronto had a lot of experienced old-timers, and we knew everyone would have to check to contain Chicago's offense. And that is just what we did, and with some great goaltending and some well-placed goals, we won.

It is necessary, of course, to score some goals along the line if a team expects to win, but the team that is going to win something more than an occasional game is the team that can check as well as score.

An excellent example of a team with more firepower than it could possibly use, yet one that lost out on the prize it wanted most, was the Boston Bruins of 1970–71. They set every kind of scoring record there was during the regular season and were overwhelming favorites to take the Stanley Cup. But after winning the first game of the quarter-finals against Montreal and taking a 5–1 lead in the second game, they fell apart.

With five goals in that game, the Bruins didn't have to score any more. All they had to do was to hold on to what they had. But they forgot to check, and Montreal scored six straight goals to win the game, 7–5. That turned the whole series around, and Boston was eliminated in that first round.

At least the Bruins learned a valuable lesson from that bitter defeat. Their checking was brilliant in the 1972 playoffs, particularly in the final series against the Rangers, and they won the Cup. New York had a well-disciplined team that was very skillful all year at passing the puck to set up good shots, but through most of the final series the Rangers were unable to get untracked against the continual checking by Boston.

The Boston line of Phil Esposito, Ken Hodge, and Wayne Cashman terrified rivals with its ability to score goals better than any line that ever preceded it in the National Hockey League. One of the important reasons for their success was their ability to forecheck.

By forechecking, a team tries to break up the other team's attack before it can even get started. It's similar to rushing the passer in football, where linemen break through in hopes of trapping the quarterback before he can line up his receiver and throw the ball.

Just as in football, though, there is a danger in hockey of getting yourself trapped if the man you are forechecking gets off a quick pass to a breaking teammate. But if a forward line is experienced and works well together, it will be only a rare occasion that it gets burned while forechecking.

The idea is to rush into the other team's end of the ice before or as soon as it takes possession of the puck. The first man in on your side doesn't go for the puck, but takes out the player with the puck, trying to ride him into the boards (see Figure 46). The second man in picks up the puck, and the third man on the line tries to set himself up in the slot or somewhere convenient where he can receive a pass and get off a good shot on the net.

When a team forechecks, it is not just one man, or one line, that presses the other team. The two defensemen also must take part in applying pressure by moving inside the blueline and being ready to participate in the attack. If they try to be too careful and play back, they're defeating the purpose that forechecking achieves by leaving too much of a gap between themselves and their forward line.

Let's go back to Esposito, Hodge, and Cashman for a moment. They're all big, rangy fellows who can hit hard, and Cashman and Hodge are particularly effective against the boards and in the corners. It isn't too uncommon to see them take the puck away from an opponent deep in his own end and set themselves up for a quick goal.

By all means, though, forechecking can be tiring on a team, and it doesn't always result in its mission of acquiring the puck. If it appears that the other team is able to set up its play and carry the puck out of its own zone, the forchecking unit must be ready to backtrack quickly and prepare to defend

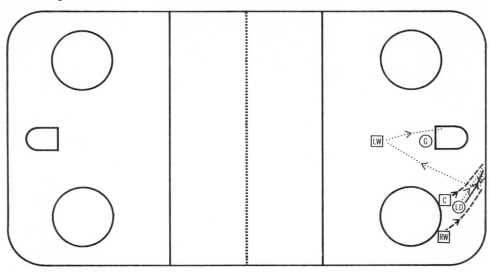

☐ = OFFENSIVE PLAYER
◯ = DEFENSIVE PLAYER
---- = PATH OF OFFENSIVE PLAYER
—— = PATH OF DEFENSIVE PLAYER
·········· = PATH OF PUCK

Figure 46. Defensive left defenseman, carrying puck, is ridden into boards by offensive center. Offensive right wing picks up puck and passes to offensive left wing, who is in slot in front of net. Offensive left wing shoots and scores.

its own goal.

The man who is the third one in, and is waiting in the slot for an opportunistic pass, also serves as the safety valve for the line, and it is his job to pick up one of the offensive breaking wingmen. If the two defensemen are also back and in position, they pick up the other forwards, which leaves every man on the attacking team covered (see Figure 47).

There are other means of forechecking, more modified versions that don't place as much stress on forcing a mistake that can be turned into a quick goal. A team can send in just one forechecker or perhaps two, with the other linemen holding back. If it is just one forechecker, usually the centerman, the wingmen come in deep, then turn and come back with the offensive wingmen, hanging on closely to their man (see Figure 48). They will stay as close to their man as possible, checking him when possible and keeping him on the outside close to the boards. If they do their job well, they will have checked that wingman out of the play.

A team may decide to forecheck at any time it wishes, but especially when it is trailing in a game and needs to score. If a team is leading, it is likely to dispense with forechecking in favor of wheeling back quickly into defensive position, with each player picking up his man as they skate back. It is a lux-

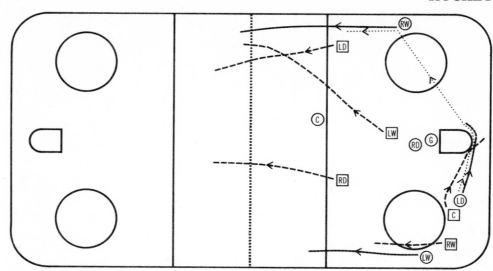

□ = OFFENSIVE PLAYER
○ = DEFENSIVE PLAYER
---- = PATH OF OFFENSIVE PLAYER
—— = PATH OF DEFENSIVE PLAYER
········· = PATH OF PUCK

Figure 47.   Offensive center and offensive right wing are trapped in deep as defensive left defenseman gets puck over to defensive right wing. Offensive left wing turns and picks up defensive right wing, and offensive left defenseman and offensive right defenseman turn and pick up their positions on defense.

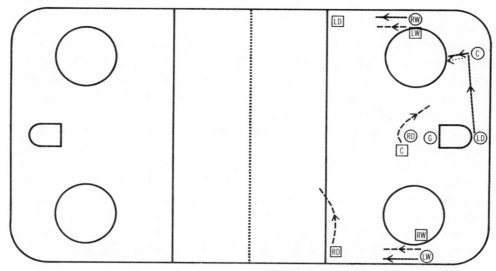

Figure 48.   Both offensive left wing and offensive right wing pick up their checks, and offensive center forechecks. If offensive center happens to get puck, offensive left wing and offensive right wing are ready to go back on the attack.

ury position of knowing you needn't score again to win the game, as long as the other team is kept off the scoreboard.

In such a situation, though, it is frequently the defensive team that winds up scoring a goal. If it is your team that is protecting the lead, and each man is quick to pick up his check, the other team can be forced into a mistake because of the pressure it is under to score a goal. By playing man to man, one of your players could be in position to pick off a pass and start the attack going the other way.

Backchecking is another form of tight defensive play that is essential to a winning effort. If your team is on offense and suddenly loses the puck, you immediately wheel around and pick up your defensive check. If you're the left wingman, you quickly turn, find the other team's right wingman, and cover him as quickly as you can. Forget the fancy, wide circles and the leisurely skate back into your own zone. You must be abrupt in your change-over and stingy with your movements.

Should your team recover the puck, forget the man you were covering. Now it's his turn to worry about you as you try to get a stride advantage over him flashing into his team's zone. But if the puck turns over again, then you reverse your gears and backcheck once more. The flow of the game is back and forth, back and forth, and you must never give the other guy a clean break simply because you were tardy in getting to your check.

While forechecking and backchecking require a total team involvement in order to be effective, there are other forms of checking, of course, that can be pursued as an individual effort.

A most common form of check is to ride the other player out of the play by using your body. However, this is not what is known as a bodycheck, a truly classic play that is not seen too much these days.

A bodycheck occurs when a defender comes out and hits someone in the middle of the ice, knocking him off his feet. It's a crushing check, and really serves to take the other man thoroughly out of the play. It is also a very difficult check to effect, and one that doesn't occur too often because you rarely can catch a skater these days who doesn't keep his head up.

One of the times a crushing bodycheck can be applied is when the skater carrying the puck is trying to get around another player and his attention is riveted on him. The defender then comes into the picture and can nail the skater good and solid and cleanly from the blind side.

A great one for doing this was Wild Bill Ezinicki, the old Toronto and Boston star. Ezinicki, in his own team's end doing his usual effective job of backchecking, would cut behind his own defenseman as the rival forward was cutting through the defense. The skater's attention would be focused on the defenseman, and before he was aware of what was happening, Ezinicki would effectively step into him (see Figure 49).

Another occasion when a good bodycheck can be applied is when a player has his head down. That makes him an easy target.

Now getting back to the point we were discussing earlier: the riding off of a player, which is a more common type of check. This is accomplished by

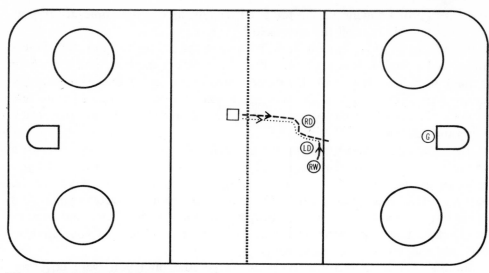

☐ = OFFENSIVE PLAYER
◯ = DEFENSIVE PLAYER
---- = PATH OF OFFENSIVE PLAYER
——— = PATH OF DEFENSIVE PLAYER
·········· = PATH OF PUCK

Figure 49. Offensive skater carrying puck tries to split defense and is creamed by defensive right wing cutting in behind defense.

angling the puckcarrier so that he has no choice but to skate toward the boards (see Figure 50). If you are defending against a skater coming down one of the wings and position yourself correctly so that he isn't able to cut through the center, he'll have to keep skating ahead, and you can ride him off at an angle until he runs out of room. Once he reaches those boards, there's nothing more he can do, and if he doesn't get rid of the puck you may be able to take it away from him or at least tie him up for a whistle. In angling a rival off, you can use your arm, your stick, and your body for support.

When you're forechecking, you might try to relieve your opponent of the puck with another useful check, the pokecheck. This simply involves reaching out with your stick in an attempt to poke the puck off an opponent's stick.

Some defenders will pokecheck at a player coming toward them, but this can be costly if your opponent is a good stickhandler. Once you've committed yourself by throwing your stick out, he can stickhandle the puck slightly off course and carry it around you. In the meantime, since you're off-balance from your check attempt, it would be difficult for you to recover in time to skate back into the play.

The hookcheck is a good check to have in your bag of tricks, but be wary of it, since it is not always the safest check, and it requires perfect timing. Often it is used as a last resort when a player knows he has been beaten by

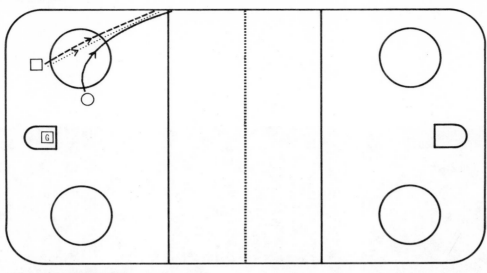

□ = OFFENSIVE PLAYER
○ = DEFENSIVE PLAYER
---- = PATH OF OFFENSIVE PLAYER
—— = PATH OF DEFENSIVE PLAYER
.... = PATH OF PUCK

Figure 50. Defensive skater angles offensive man into boards and takes puck away.

the puckcarrier and has to stretch ahead with his stick in a final attempt to break up the attack.

If a rival player has the puck, you can come up from behind him, reach out, hook the puck off his stick, and be going back the other way before he realizes he's lost the puck.

The term "hooking" also can mean catching onto a rival player with your stick and getting a free ride.

Among the more popular hooking areas are the leg, the shinguard on the leg or knee, the leg of the pants, around the waist, around the stick, and around the glove.

There is an art to hooking and not being called for it by the referee, and this marks the difference between your star player and an inexperienced player. Many star players have become proficient at reaching after a player who has the jump on them, hooking onto a piece of equipment, and with this little boost pulling themselves ahead while drawing the puckcarrier back toward them. Once they've narrowed the gap sufficiently, they let go before the hooking violation has become flagrant.

They know they've accomplished their purpose, and there's no need to look for trouble. An inexperienced player, though, will make his hook more obvious and will maintain it longer than is necessary. For this reason, he will be

penalized where a better player than he is won't be sent off for what amounts to a similar infraction. But it's not a question of the referee discriminating against a poorer player in favor of a star, it's simply a matter of a good player being rink-wise enough to understand just what he can get away with.

If you want an example of a star player who became proficient at hooking —and getting away with it—you need look no farther than Gordie Howe.

However it is done, checking is as essential on a winning team as scoring. Many players, although they are overlooked by the general fan because they are not scorers, have enjoyed productive careers in the National Hockey League because of their ability to check. A couple of old friends who come to mind are Floyd Curry of Montreal and Marty Pavelich of Detroit.

Curry never seemed to get many points during the year, although he contributed his share to a number of championship teams with his checking ability, but quite often in the playoffs he was the one who would come up with the key goals. Pavelich performed along the same lines, never scoring much himself but checking hard and containing the top scorers on the other club.

These players, and many others, took great delight in their checking ability and got as much kick out of stopping someone else from scoring as they did from scoring themselves.

Your most valuable player, of course, the superstar, is the all-around player who is both a high scorer and a top checker.

RULES INTRODUCTION

On the following pages you will find excerpts from the official 1975–76 National Hockey League rule book. We are presenting those portions that are most pertinent to the actual playing of the game.

There is only a slight variance between NHL rules and those of the Amateur Hockey Association of the United States (AHAUS), the organization that governs the local leagues and clubs, that regulates the participation of virtually every hockey-playing youngster who reads this instructional book. As expressed by Hal Trumble, referee-in-chief of the AHAUS, "We make a very definite effort to keep our rules the same [as the NHL's] because we feel it is better for the sport as a whole. It becomes easier for both the players and the fans to understand, whereas if there were a number of differences, it would only cause confusion."

We do point out, however, that there is a significant difference between the amateur rules and those of the National Collegiate Athletic Association, which governs the varsity programs of U.S. colleges and high schools. The most notable divergence is the absence of the center redline in the NCAA jurisdiction, but there is no need to differentiate any further inasmuch as those youngsters joining school teams will be well introduced to those rules.

A large portion of the difference between pro and AHAUS rules stems from the simple fact that the amateur programs can't match the affluence of the NHL teams. For example, the NHL requires a specific size rink while the AHAUS doesn't, and the National League has mandatory requirements for the location of the penalty box, the size of the players' benches, the responsibilities of minor officials, and the presence of an official scorer for each game. These, of course, are luxuries local leagues cannot afford.

As far as playing rules, one basic difference is in the area of icing the puck. According to AHAUS rules, icing occurs the moment the puck crosses the goal line. In the NHL, the puck first must be touched by a defensive player.

Another difference concerns the offside pass; the amateur ruling is the same as that used in international competition and is intended to open up the game a bit. If a pass from the defensive zone precedes a player who was in the neutral zone across the center redline, no offside violation will occur and that player is eligible to play the puck.

Here's a caution for those rambunctious youngsters who watch the pros fight and feel they'd like to give it a go. Remember, fighting costs a pro only five minutes, and it's likely he'll take an opponent with him into the penalty box, so the cost to his team might be minimal. But on the amateur level, a player who receives a major penalty for fighting is automatically out of that game and also is ineligible to play in his team's next game. Think about it, and you'll realize it's better to keep a cool head.

The rules are just as harsh when it comes to a game misconduct penalty. The guilty player is automatically suspended for the next game as well.

Players aren't fined on the amateur level, as are the wealthier pros, but local authorities have discretionary power to impose suspensions.

The National Hockey League makes available, for 50¢ plus any applicable sales tax, copies of its rule book. These can be obtained by sending the money and writing to:

Bob Casey
Public Relations Director
National Hockey League
Suite 2480
2 Pennsylvania Plaza
New York, N.Y. 10001

PENALTIES

Rule 26. Penalties

Penalties shall be actual playing time and shall be divided into the following classes:

    (1) Minor Penalties
    (2) Bench Minor Penalties
    (3) Major Penalties
    (4) Misconduct Penalties
    (5) Match Penalties
    (6) Penalty Shot.

Where coincident penalties are imposed on players of both teams the penalized players of the visiting team shall take their positions on the penalty bench first in the place designated for visiting players.

(NOTE) *When play is not actually in progress and an offense is committed by any player, the same penalty shall apply as though play were actually in progress.*

Rule 27. Minor Penalties

(a) For a "MINOR PENALTY," any player, other than a goalkeeper, shall be ruled off the ice for two minutes during which time no substitute shall be permitted.

(b) A "BENCH MINOR" penalty involves the removal from the ice of one player of the team against which the penalty is awarded for a period of two minutes. Any player except a goalkeeper of the team may be designated to serve the penalty by the Manager or Coach through the playing Captain and such player shall take his place on the penalty bench promptly and serve the penalty as if it was a minor penalty imposed upon him.

(c) If while a team is "short-handed" by one or more minor or bench minor penalties the opposing team scores a goal, the first of such penalties shall automatically terminate.

(NOTE 1) *"Short-handed" means that the team must be below the numerical strength of its opponents on the ice at the time the goal is scored. The minor or bench minor penalty which terminates automatically is the one which causes the team scored against to be "short-handed" originally (first penalty). Thus coincident minor penalties to both teams do NOT cause either side to be "short-handed."*

This rule shall also apply when a goal is scored on a penalty shot.

When the minor penalties of two players of the same team terminate at the same time the Captain of that team shall designate to the Referee which of such players will return to the ice first and the Referee will instruct the Penalty Timekeeper accordingly.

When a player receives a major penalty and a minor penalty at the same time the major penalty shall be served first by the penalized player except under Rule 28 (c) in which case the minor penalty will be recorded and served first.

(NOTE 2) *This applies to the case where BOTH penalties are imposed on the SAME player.*

See also Note to Rule 33.

Rule 28.   Major Penalties

(a) For the first "MAJOR PENALTY" in any one game, the offender, except the goalkeeper, shall be ruled off the ice for five minutes, during which time no substitute shall be permitted. . . .

(b) For the third major penalty in the same game, to the same player, he shall be ruled off the ice for the balance of the playing time, but a substitute shall be permitted to replace the player so suspended after five minutes shall have elapsed. . . .

(c) When coincident major penalties or coincident penalties of equal duration, including a major penalty, are imposed against players of both teams, the penalized players shall all take their places on the penalty benches and such penalized players shall not leave the penalty bench until the first stoppage of play following the expiry of their respective penalties. Immediate substitutions shall be made for an equal number of major penalties or *coincident penalties of equal duration including a major penalty* to each team so penalized and the penalties of the players for which substitution have been made shall not be taken into account for the purpose of the delayed Rule 33.

Where it is required to determine which of the penalized players shall be designated to serve the delayed penalty under Rule 33 the penalized team shall have the right to make such designation not in conflict with Rule 27.

Rule 29. Misconduct Penalties

(a) "MISCONDUCT" penalties to all players except the goalkeeper involve removal from the game for a period of ten minutes each. A substitute player is permitted to immediately replace a player serving a misconduct penalty. A player whose misconduct penalty has expired shall remain in the penalty box until the next stoppage of play.

When a player receives a minor penalty and a misconduct penalty at the same time, the penalized team shall immediately put a substitute player on the penalty bench and he shall serve the minor penalty without change.

When a player receives a major penalty and a misconduct penalty at the same time, the penalized team shall place a substitute player on the penalty bench before the major penalty expires and no replacement for the penalized player shall be permitted to enter the game except from the penalty bench. Any violation of this provision shall be treated as an illegal substitution . . . calling for a bench minor penalty. . . .

(c) A "GAME MISCONDUCT" penalty involves the suspension of a player for the balance of the game but a substitute is permitted to replace immediately the player so removed. . . . [The] case shall be reported to the President who shall have full power to impose such further penalties by way of suspension . . . on the penalized player or any other player involved in the altercation.

(NOTE) *For all "Game Misconduct" penalties regardless of when imposed, a total of ten minutes shall be charged in the records against the offending player.*

(d) A Game Misconduct penalty shall be imposed on any player or goalkeeper on the ice who is the first to intervene in an altercation then in progress. This penalty is in addition to any other penalty incurred in the same incident.

Rule 30. Match Penalties

(a) A "MATCH" penalty involves the suspension of a player for the balance of the game, and the offender shall be ordered to the dressing room immediately. A substitute player is permitted to replace the penalized player after ten minutes playing time has elapsed when the penalty is imposed under Rule 49, and after five minutes actual playing time has elapsed when the penalty is imposed under Rule 44.

(NOTE 1) *Regulations regarding additional penalties and substitutes are specifically covered in individual Rules 44, 49 and 64; any additional penalty shall be served by a player to be designated by the Manager or Coach of the offending team through the playing Captain, such player to take his place in the penalty box immediately.*

For all "MATCH" penalties, regardless of when imposed, or prescribed additional penalties, a total of ten minutes shall be charged in the records against the offending player.

(NOTE 2) *When coincident match penalties have been imposed under Rule 44, Rule 49 or Rule 64 to a player on both teams Rule 28 (c) covering coincident major penalties will be applicable with respect to player substitution.*

(b) . . . [The] case shall be investigated promptly by the President who shall have full power to impose such further penalty by way of suspension . . . on the penalized player or any other player involved in the altercation.

(NOTE) *The Referee is required to report all match penalties and the surrounding circumstances to the President of the League immediately following the game in which they occur.*

Rule 31. Penalty Shot

(a) Any infraction of the rules which calls for a "Penalty Shot" shall be taken as follows:

The Referee shall cause to be announced . . . the name of the player designated by him or selected by the team entitled to take the shot (as appropriate) and shall then place the puck on the center face-off spot and the player taking the shot will, on the instruction of the Referee, play the puck from there and shall attempt to score on the goalkeeper. The player taking the shot may carry the puck in any part of the Neutral Zone or his own Defending Zone but once the puck has crossed the Attacking Blue Line it must be kept in motion towards the opponent's goal line and once it is shot the play shall be considered complete. No goal can be scored on a rebound of any kind and any time the puck crosses the goal line the shot shall be considered complete.

Only a player designated as a Goalkeeper or Alternate Goalkeeper may defend against the penalty shot.

(b) The Goalkeeper must remain in his crease until the player taking the penalty shot has touched the puck and in the event of violation of this rule or any foul committed by a goalkeeper the Referee shall allow the shot to be taken and if the shot fails he shall permit the penalty shot to be taken over again.

The goalkeeper may attempt to stop the shot in any manner except by throwing his stick or any object, in which case a goal shall be awarded.

(NOTE) *See Rule 80.*

(c) In cases where a penalty shot has been awarded under Rule 62(g)·—Interference, under Rule 66(k)—for illegal entry into the game, under Rule 80(a)—for throwing a stick and under Rule 83 (b)—for fouling from behind, the Referee shall designate the player who has been fouled as the player who shall take the penalty shot.

In cases where a penalty shot has been awarded [because of] deliberate illegal substitution with insufficient playing time remaining—or [under] Rule 50 (c)—deliberately displacing goal post or Rule 53 (c)—falling on the puck in the crease or Rule 57 (d)—picking up the puck from the crease area—the penalty shot shall be taken by a player selected by the Captain of the non-offending team from the players on the ice at the time when the foul was committed. Such selection shall be reported to the Referee and cannot be changed.

If by reason of injury the player designated by the Referee to take the penalty shot is unable to do so within a reasonable time, the shot may be taken by a player selected by the Captain of the non-offending team from the players on the ice when the foul was committed. Such selection shall be reported to the Referee and cannot be changed.

(d) Should the player in respect to whom a penalty shot has been awarded himself commit a foul in connection with the same play or circumstances, either before or after the penalty shot penalty has been awarded . . . he shall first be permitted to do so before being sent to the penalty bench to serve the penalty except when such a penalty is for a game misconduct or match penalty in which case the penalty shot shall be taken by a player selected by the Captain of the non-offending team from the players on the ice at the time when the foul was committed.

If at the time a penalty shot is awarded the goalkeeper of the penalized team has been removed from the ice to substitute another player the goalkeeper shall be permitted to return to the ice before the penalty shot is taken.

(e) While the penalty shot is being taken, players of both sides shall withdraw to the sides of the rink and beyond the center red line.

(f) If, while the penalty shot is being taken, any player of the opposing team shall have by some action interfered with or distracted the player taking the shot and because of such action the shot should have failed, a second attempt shall be permitted and the Referee shall impose a misconduct penalty on the player so interfering or distracting.

(g) If a goal is scored from a penalty shot the puck shall be faced at center ice in the usual way. If a goal is not scored the puck shall be faced at either of the end face-off spots in the zone in which the penalty shot has been tried.

(h) Should a goal be scored from a penalty shot, a further penalty to the offending player shall not be applied unless the offense for which the penalty shot was awarded was such as to incur a major or match penalty or misconduct penalty, in which case the penalty prescribed for the particular offense shall be imposed.

  If the offense for which the penalty shot was awarded was such as would normally incur a minor penalty, then regardless of whether the penalty shot results in a goal or not, no further minor penalty shall be served.

(i) If the foul upon which the penalty shot is based occurs during actual playing time the penalty shot shall be awarded and taken immediately in the usual manner notwithstanding any delay occasioned by a slow whistle by the Referee to permit the play to be completed which delay results in the expiry of the regular playing time in any period.

  The time required for the taking of a penalty shot shall not be included in the regular playing time or any overtime.

Rule 32. Goalkeeper's Penalties

(a) A goalkeeper shall not be sent to the penalty bench for an offense which incurs a minor penalty, but instead the minor penalty shall be served by another member of his team who was on the ice when the offense was committed, said player to be designated by the Manager or Coach of the offending team through the playing Captain and such substitute shall not be changed.

(b) Same as 32 (a) above except change "minor" to "major."

(c) Should a goalkeeper incur three major penalties in one game he shall be ruled off the ice for the balance of the playing time and his place will be taken by a member of his own Club, or by a regular substitute goalkeeper who is available. . . .

(d) Should a goalkeeper on the ice incur a misconduct penalty this penalty shall be served by another member of his team who was on the ice when the offense was committed, said player to be designated by the Manager or Coach of the offending team through the playing Captain . . .

(e) Should a goalkeeper incur a game misconduct penalty, his place then will be taken by a member of his own club, or by a regular substitute goalkeeper who is available, and such player will be allowed the goalkeeper's full equipment. . . .

(f) Should a goalkeeper incur a match penalty, his place then will be taken by a member of his own club, or by a substitute goalkeeper who is available, and such player will be allowed the goalkeeper's equipment. However, any additional penalties as specifically called for by the individual rules covering match penalties will apply, and the offending team shall be penalized accordingly; such additional penalty to be served by another member of the team on the ice at the time the offense was committed, said player to be designated by the Manager or Coach of the offending team through the playing Captain. (See Rules 44, 49 and 64).

(g) . . . [The] case shall be investigated promptly by the President who shall have full power to impose such further penalty by way of suspension . . . on the penalized goalkeeper or any other player in the altercation.

(h) A minor penalty shall be imposed on a goalkeeper who leaves the immediate vicinity of his crease during an altercation. In addition . . . this incident shall be reported to the President for such further disciplinary action as may be required.

(NOTE) *All penalties imposed on goalkeeper, regardless of who serves penalty or any substitution, shall be charged in the records against the goalkeeper.*

(i) If a goalkeeper participates in the play in any manner when he is beyond the center red line a minor penalty shall be imposed upon him.

Rule 33.   Delayed Penalties

(a) If a third player of any team shall be penalized while two players of the same team are serving penalties, the penalty time of the third player shall not commence until the penalty time of one of the two players already penalized shall have elapsed. Nevertheless, the third player penalized must at once proceed to the penalty bench but may be replaced by a substitute until such time as the penalty time of the penalized player shall commence.

(b) When any team shall have three players serving penalties at the same time and because of the delayed penalty rule, a substitute for the third offender is on the ice, none of the three penalized players on the penalty bench may return to the ice until play has been stopped. When play has been stopped, the

player whose full penalty has expired may return to the play.

Provided however that the Penalty Timekeeper shall permit the return to the ice in the order of expiry of their penalties, of a player or players when by reason of the expiration of their penalties the penalized team is entitled to have more than four players on the ice.

(c) In the case of delayed penalties, the Referee shall instruct the Penalty Timekeeper that penalized players whose penalties have expired shall only be allowed to return to the ice when there is a stoppage of play.

When the penalties of two players of the same team will expire at the same time the Captain of that team will designate to the Referee which of such players will return to the ice first and the Referee will instruct the Penalty Timekeeper accordingly.

When a major and a minor penalty are imposed at the same time on players of the same team the Penalty Timekeeper shall record the minor as being the first of such penalties.

(NOTE) *This applies to the case where the two penalties are imposed on DIFFERENT players of the same team. See also Note to Rule 27.*

Rule 34.   Calling of Penalties

(a) Should an infraction of the rules which would call for a minor, major, misconduct, game misconduct or match penalty be committed by a player of the side in possession of the puck, the Referee shall immediately blow his whistle and give the penalties to the deserving players.

The resulting face-off shall be

made at the place where the play was stopped unless the stoppage occurs in the Attacking Zone of the player penalized in which case the face-off shall be made at the nearest face-off spot in the Neutral Zone.

(b) Should an infraction of the rules which would call for a minor, major, misconduct, game misconduct or match penalty be committed by a player of the team not in possession of the puck, the Referee will blow his whistle and impose the penalty on the offending player upon completion of the play by the team in possession of the puck.

(NOTE) *There shall be no signal given by the Referee for a misconduct or Game Misconduct penalty under this section.*

The resulting face-off shall be made at the place where the play was stopped, unless during the period of a delayed whistle due to a foul by a player of the side NOT in possession, the side in possession ices the puck, shoots the puck so that it goes out of bounds or is unplayable, then the face-off following the stoppage shall take place in the Neutral Zone near the Defending Blue Line of the team shooting the puck.

If the penalty or penalties to be imposed are minor penalties and a goal is scored on the play by the non-offending side the minor penalty or penalties shall not be imposed but major and match penalties shall be imposed in the nor-mal manner regardless of whether a goal is scored or not.

(NOTE 1) *"Completion of the play by the team in possession" in this rule means that the puck must have come into the possession and control of an opposing player or has been "frozen." This does* not *mean a rebound off the goalkeeper, the goal or the boards or any accidental contact with the body or equipment of an opposing player.*

(NOTE 2) *If after the Referee has signaled a penalty but before the whistle has been blown the puck shall enter the goal of the non-offending team as the direct result of the action of a player of that team, the goal shall be allowed and the penalty signaled shall be imposed in the normal manner.*

If when a team is "short-handed" by reason of one or more minor or bench minor penalties the Referee signals a further minor penalty or penalties against the "short-handed" team and a goal is scored by the non-offending side before the whistle is blown then the goal shall be allowed, the penalty or penalties signaled shall be washed out and the first of the minor penalties already being served shall automatically terminate under Rule 27 (c).

(c) Should the same offending player commit other fouls on the same play, either before or after the Referee has blown his whistle, the offending player shall serve such penalties consecutively.

PLAYING RULES

Rule 42. Abuse of Officials and Other Misconduct

(NOTE) *In the enforcement of this rule the Referee has, in many instances, the option of imposing a "misconduct penalty" or a "bench minor penalty." In principle the Referee is directed to impose a "bench minor penalty" in respect to the violations which occur on or in the immediate vicinity of the players' bench but off the playing surface, and in all cases affecting non-playing personnel or players. A "misconduct penalty" should be imposed for violations which occur on the playing surface or in the penalty bench area and where the penalized player is readily identifiable.*

(a) A misconduct penalty shall be imposed on any player who uses obscene, profane or abusive language to any person or who intentionally knocks or shoots the puck out of the reach of an official who is retrieving it or who deliberately throws any equipment out of the playing area.

(b) A minor penalty shall be assessed to any player who challenges or disputes the rulings of any official during a game. If the player persists in such challenge or dispute he shall be assessed a misconduct penalty and any further dispute will result in a Game Misconduct Penalty being assessed to the offending player.

(c) A misconduct penalty shall be imposed on any player or players who bang the boards with their sticks or other instruments any time.

In the event that the Coach, Trainer, Manager or Club Executive commits an infraction under this Rule a bench minor penalty shall be imposed.

(d) A bench minor penalty shall be imposed on the team of any penalized player who does not proceed directly and immediately to the penalty box and take his place on the penalty bench or to the dressing room when so ordered by the referee.

Where coincident penalties are imposed on players of both teams the penalized players of the visiting team shall take their positions on the penalty bench first in the place designated for visiting players, or where there is no special designation then on the bench farthest from the gate. . . .

(e) A misconduct penalty shall be imposed on any player who, after warning by the Referee, persists in any course of conduct (including threatening or abusive language or gestures or similar actions) designed to incite an opponent into incurring a penalty.

If, after the assessment of a Misconduct Penalty a player persists in any course of conduct for which he was previously assessed a Misconduct Penalty, he shall be assessed a Game Misconduct Penalty.

(f) In the case of any Club Executive, Manager, Coach or Trainer being guilty of such misconduct, he is to be removed from the bench by order of the Referee, and his case reported to the President for further action.

(g) If any Club Executive, Manager, Coach or Trainer is removed from the bench by order of the Referee, he must not sit near the bench of his club, nor in any way direct or attempt to direct the play of his club.

(i) A bench minor penalty shall be imposed against the offending team if any player, any Club Executive, Manager, Coach or Trainer uses obscene, profane or abusive language or gesture to any person or uses the name of any official coupled with any vociferous remarks.

(j) A bench minor penalty shall be imposed against the offending team if any player, Trainer, Coach, Manager or Club Executive in the vicinity of the players' bench or penalty bench throws anything on the ice during the progress of the game or during stoppage of play.

(NOTE) *The penalty provided under this rule is in addition to any penalty imposed under Rule 46 (c) "Broken Stick."*

(k) A bench minor penalty shall be imposed against the offending team if any player, Trainer, Coach, Manager or Club Executive interferes in any manner with any game official including Referee, Linesmen, Timekeepers or Goal Judges in the performance of their duties.

The Referee may assess further penalties under Rule 67 (Molesting Officials) if he deems them to be warranted.

(l) A misconduct penalty shall be imposed on any player or players who, except for the purpose of taking their positions on the penalty bench, enter or remain in the Referee's Crease while he is reporting to or consulting with any game official including Linesmen, Timekeeper, Penalty Timekeeper, Official Scorer or Announcer.

Rule 43. Adjustment to Clothing and Equipment

(a) Play shall not be stopped, nor the game delayed by reason of adjustments to clothing, equipment, shoes, skates or sticks.

For an infringement of this rule, a minor penalty shall be given.

(b) The onus of maintaining clothing and equipment in proper condition shall be upon the player. If adjustments are required, the player shall retire from the ice and play shall continue uninterruptedly with a substitute.

(c) No delay shall be permitted for the repair or adjustment of goalkeeper's equipment. If adjustments are required the goalkeeper will retire from the ice and his place will be taken by the substitute goalkeeper immediately and no warm-up will be permitted.

(d) For an infraction of this rule by a goalkeeper, a minor penalty shall be imposed.

Rule 44.   Attempt to Injure

(a) A match penalty shall be imposed on any player who deliberately attempts to injure an opponent and the circumstances shall be reported to the President for further action. A substitute for the penalized player shall be permitted at the end of the fifth minute.

(b) A Game Misconduct penalty shall be imposed on any player who deliberately attempts to injure an Official, Manager, Coach or Trainer in any manner and the circumstances shall be reported to the President for further action.

(NOTE) *The president, upon preliminary investigation indicating the probable imposition of supplementary disciplinary action, may order the immediate suspension of a player who has incurred a match penalty under this rule, pending the final determination of such supplementary disciplinary action.*

Rule 45.   Board-Checking

A minor or major penalty, at the discretion of the Referee based upon the degree of violence of the impact with the boards, shall be imposed on any player who bodychecks, cross-checks, elbows, charges or trips an opponent in such a manner that causes the opponent to be thrown violently into the boards.

(NOTE) *Any unnecessary contact with a player playing the puck on an obvious "icing" or "off-side" play which results in that player being knocked into the fence is "boarding" and must be penalized as such. In other instances where there is no contact with the fence it should be treated as "charging."*

"Rolling" an opponent (if he is the puck carrier) along the fence where he is endeavoring to go through too small an opening is not boarding. However, if the opponent is not the puck carrier, then such action should be penalized as boarding, charging, interference or if the arms or stick are employed it should be called holding or hooking.

Rule 46.   Broken Stick

(a) A player without a stick may participate in the game. A player whose stick is broken may participate in the game provided he drops the broken portion. A minor penalty shall be imposed for an infraction of this rule.

(NOTE) *A broken stick is one which, in the opinion of the Referee, is unfit for normal play.*

(b) A goalkeeper may continue to play with a broken stick until stoppage of play or until he has been legally provided with a stick.

(c) A player whose stick is broken may not receive a stick thrown on to the ice from any part of the rink but must obtain same at his players' bench. A goalkeeper whose stick is broken may not receive a stick thrown on to the ice from any part of the rink but may receive a stick from a teammate without proceeding to his players' bench. A minor penalty plus a misconduct penalty shall be imposed on the player or goalkeeper receiving a stick illegally under this rule.

(d) A goalkeeper whose stick is broken may not go to the players' bench for a replacement but must receive his stick from a teammate.

For an infraction of this rule a minor penalty shall be imposed on the goalkeeper.

Rule 47.   Charging

(a) A minor or major penalty shall be imposed on a player who runs or jumps into or charges an opponent. . . .

(c) A minor or major penalty shall be imposed on a player who charges a goalkeeper while the goalkeeper is within his goal crease.

(NOTE) *If more than two steps or strides are taken it shall be considered a charge.*

A goalkeeper is NOT "fair game" just because he is outside the goal crease area. A penalty for interference or charging (minor or major) should be called in every case where an opposing player makes unnecessary contact with a goalkeeper.

Likewise Referees should be alert to penalize goalkeepers for tripping, slashing or spearing in the vicinity of the goal.

Rule 48.   Cross-Checking and
Butt-Ending

(a) A minor or major penalty, at the discretion of the Referee, shall be imposed on a player who "cross-checks" an opponent.

(b) A major penalty shall be imposed on any player who "butt-ends" or attempts to "butt-end" an opponent.

(NOTE) *Attempt to "butt-end" shall include all cases where a "butt-end" gesture is made regardless whether body contact is made or not. . . .*

(NOTE) *Cross-check shall mean a check delivered with both hands on the stick and no part of the stick on the ice.*

Rule 49.   Deliberate Injury of Opponents

(a) A match penalty shall be imposed on a player who deliberately injures an opponent in any manner.

(NOTE) *Any player wearing tape or any other material on his hands who cuts or injures an opponent during an altercation shall receive a match penalty under this rule. . . .*

(c) No substitute shall be permitted to take the place of the penalized player until ten minutes actual playing time shall have elapsed, from the time the penalty was imposed.

(d) A Game Misconduct penalty shall be imposed on any player who deliberately injures an Official, Manager, Coach or Trainer in any manner and the circumstances shall be reported to the President for further action.

(e) A match penalty shall be imposed on any player who deliberately "head-butts" or attempts to "head-butt" an opponent during an altercation and the circumstances shall be reported to the President for further action. A substitute shall be permitted at the end of the fifth minute. In the event there is an injury to an opponent resulting from

the foul no substitute shall be permitted to take the place of the penalized player until ten minutes actual playing shall be elapsed.

(NOTE) *The president, upon preliminary investigation indicating the probable imposition of supplementary disciplinary action, may order the immediate suspension of a player who has incurred a match penalty under this rule, pending the final determination of such supplementary disciplinary action.*

Rule 50.   Delaying the Game

(a) A minor penalty shall be imposed on any player or goalkeeper who delays the game by deliberately shooting or batting the puck with his stick outside the playing area.

(NOTE) *This penalty shall apply also when a player or goalkeeper deliberately bats or shoots the puck with his stick outside the playing area after a stoppage of play.*

(b) A minor penalty shall be imposed on any player or goalkeeper who throws or deliberately bats the puck with his hand or stick outside the playing area.

(c) A minor penalty shall be imposed on any player (including goalkeeper) who delays the game by deliberately displacing a goal post from its normal position. The Referee or linesmen shall stop play immediately when a goal post has been displaced.

If the goal post is deliberately displaced by a goalkeeper or player during the course of a "breakaway" a penalty shot will be awarded to the non-offending team, which shot shall be taken by the player last in possession of the puck.

(NOTE) *A player with a "breakaway" is defined as a player in con-*

trol of the puck with no oppposition between him and the opposing goal and with a reasonable scoring opportunity.

If by reason of insufficient time in the regular playing time or by reason of penalties already imposed the minor penalty awarded to a player for deliberately displacing his own goal post cannot be served in its entirety within the regular playing time of the game or at any time in overtime, a penalty shot shall be awarded against the offending team.

(d) A bench minor penalty shall be imposed upon any team which, after warning by the Referee to its Captain or Alternate Captain to place the correct number of players on the ice and commence play, fails to comply with the Referee's direction and thereby causes any delay by making additional substitutions, by persisting in having its players off-side, or in any other manner.

Rule 51. Elbowing and Kneeing

(a) A minor or major penalty, at the discretion of the Referee, shall be imposed on any player who uses his elbow or knee in such a manner as to in any way foul an opponent. . . .

Rule 52.   Face-Offs

(a) The puck shall be "faced-off" by the Referee or the Linesman dropping the puck on the ice between the sticks of the players "facing-off." Players facing-off will stand squarely facing their opponents' end of the rink approximately one stick length apart with the blades of their sticks on the ice.

When the face-off takes place in any of the end face-off circles the players taking part shall take their positions so that they will have one skate on each side and clear of the line running through the face-off spot and with both feet behind and clear of the line parallel to the goal line. The sticks of both players facing-off shall have the blades on the ice and entirely clear of the spot or place where the puck is to be dropped.

No other player shall be allowed to enter the face-off circle or come within fifteen feet of the players facing-off the puck, and must stand on side on all face-offs.

If a violation of this sub-section of this rule occurs the Referee or Linesman shall re-face the puck.

(b) If after warning by the Referee or Linesman either of the players fails to take his proper position for the face-off promptly, the official shall be entitled to face-off the puck notwithstanding such default.

(c) In the conduct of any face-off anywhere on the playing surface no player facing-off shall make any physical contact with his opponent's body by means of his own body or by his stick except in the course of playing the puck after the face-off has been completed.

For violation of this rule the Referee shall impose a minor penalty or penalties on the player(s) whose action(s) caused the physical contact.

(NOTE) *"Conduct of any face-off" commences when the Referee designates the place of the face-off and he (or the Linesman) takes up his position to drop the puck.*

(d) If a player facing-off fails to take his proper position immediately when directed by the Official, the Official may order him replaced for that face-off by any teammate then on the ice.

No substitution of players shall

be permitted until the face-off has been completed and play has been resumed.

(e) A second violation of any of the provisions of sub-section (a) hereof by the same team during the same face-off shall be penalized with a minor penalty to the player who commits the second violation of the rule.

(f) When an infringement of a rule has been committed or a stoppage of play has been caused by any player of the attacking side in the Attacking Zone the ensuing face-off shall be made in the Neutral Zone on the nearest face-off spot.

(NOTE) *This includes stoppage of play caused by player of attacking side shooting the puck on to the back of the defending team's net without any intervening action by the defending team.*

(g) When an infringement of a rule has been committed by players of both sides in the play resulting in the stoppage, the ensuing face-off will be made at the place of such infringement or at the place where play is stopped.

(h) When stoppage occurs between the end face-off spots and near end of rink the puck shall be faced-off at the end face-off spot, on the side where the stoppage occurs unless otherwise expressly provided by these rules.

(i) No face-off shall be made within fifteen feet of the goal or sideboards.

(j) When a goal is illegally scored as a result of a puck being deflected directly from an official anywhere in the defending zone the resulting face-off shall be made at the end face-off spot in the defending zone.

(k) When the game is stopped for any reason not specifically covered in the official rules, the puck must be faced-off where it was last played.

(l) The whistle will not be blown by the official to start play. Playing time will commence from the instant the puck is faced-off and will stop when the whistle is blown.

Rule 53.   Falling on Puck

(a) A minor penalty shall be imposed on a player other than the goalkeeper who deliberately falls on or gathers a puck into his body.

(NOTE) *Any player who drops to his knees to block shots should not be penalized if the puck is shot under [him] or becomes lodged in [his] clothing or equipment but any use of the hands to make the puck unplayable should be penalized promptly.*

(b) A minor penalty shall be imposed on a goalkeeper who (when his body is entirely outside the boundaries of his own crease area and when the puck is behind the goal line) deliberately falls on or gathers the puck into his body or who holds or places the puck against the boards.

(c) No defending player, except the goalkeeper, will be permitted to fall on the puck or hold the puck or gather a puck into the body or hands when the puck is within the goal crease.

For infringement of this rule, play shall immediately be stopped and a penalty shot shall be ordered against the offending team, but no other penalty shall be given.

(NOTE) *This rule shall be interpreted so that a penalty shot will be awarded only when the puck is in the crease at the instant the offense occurs. However, in cases where the puck is outside the crease, Rule 53 (a) may still apply and a minor penalty may be imposed, even though no penalty shot is awarded.*

Rule 54.   Fisticuffs

(a) A major, double minor or minor penalty at the discretion of the Referee shall be imposed on any player who starts fisticuffs.

(b) A minor penalty shall be imposed on a player who, having been struck, shall retaliate with a blow or attempted blow. However, at the discretion of the Referee a major or a double minor penalty may be imposed if such player continues the altercation.

(NOTE 1) *The Referee is provided very wide latitude in the penalties which he may impose under this rule. This is done intentionally to enable him to differentiate between the obvious degrees of responsibility of the participants either for starting the fighting or persisting in continuing the fighting. The discretion provided should be exercised realistically.*

(NOTE 2) *Referees are directed to employ every means provided by these Rules to stop "brawling" and should use Rule 42 (c) for this purpose.*

(c) A Misconduct or Game Misconduct penalty shall be imposed on any player involved in fisticuffs off the playing surface or with another player who is off the playing surface.

(d) A Game Misconduct penalty shall be imposed on any player or goalkeeper on the ice who is the first to intervene in an altercation then in progress. This penalty is in addition to any other penalty incurred in the same incident.

Rule 55.   Goals and Assists

(NOTE) *It is the responsibility of the Official Scorer to award goals and assists, and his decision in this respect is final notwithstanding the report of the Referee or any other game official. Such awards shall be made or withheld strictly in accordance with the provisions of this rule. Therefore, it is essential that the Official Scorer shall be thoroughly familiar with every aspect of this rule, be alert to observe all actions which could affect the making of an award and, above all, the awards must be made or withheld with absolute impartiality.*

In case of an obvious error in awarding a goal or an assist which has been announced, it should be corrected promptly but changes should not be made in the official scoring summary after the Referee has signed the Game Report.

(a) A goal shall be scored when the puck shall have been put between the goal posts by the stick of a player of the attacking side, from in front, and below the cross bar, and entirely across a red line, the width of the diameter of the goal posts drawn on the ice from one goal post to the other.

(b) A goal shall be scored if the puck is put into the goal in any way by a player of the defending side. The player of the attacking side who last played the puck shall be credited with the goal but no assist shall be awarded.

(c) If an attacking player kicks the puck and it is deflected into the net by any player of the defending side except the goalkeeper, the goal shall be allowed. The player who kicked the puck shall be credited with the goal but no assist shall be awarded.

(d) If the puck shall have been deflected into the goal from the shot of an attacking player by striking any part of the person of a player of the same side, a goal shall be allowed. The player who deflected the puck shall be credited with the goal. The goal shall not be allowed if the puck has been kicked, thrown or otherwise deliberately directed into the goal by any means other than a stick.

(e) If a goal is scored as a result of a puck being deflected directly into the net from an official the goal shall not be allowed.

(f) Should a player legally propel a puck into the goal crease of the opponent club and the puck should become loose and available to another player of the attacking side, a goal scored on the play shall be legal.

(g) Any goal scored, other than as covered by the official rules, shall not be allowed.

(h) A "goal" shall be credited in the scoring records to a player who shall have propelled the puck into the opponents' goal. Each "goal" shall count one point in the player's record.

(i) When a player scores a goal an "assist" shall be credited to the player or players taking part in the play immediately preceding the goal, but not more than two assists can be given on any goal. Each "assist" so credited shall count one point in the player's record.

(j) Only one point can be credited to any one player on a goal.

Rule 56.   Gross Misconduct

(a) The Referee may suspend from the game and order to the dressing room for the remainder of the game any player, Manager, Coach, or Trainer guilty of gross misconduct of any kind.

(b) If a player so dismissed is taking part in the game, he shall be charged with a game misconduct penalty, and a substitute shall be permitted.

(c) The Referee in charge is to decide on any violation and report the incident to the President of the League for further action.

Rule 57.   Handling Puck with Hands

(a) If a player, except the goalkeeper, closes his hand on the puck the play shall be stopped and a minor penalty shall be imposed on him. A goalkeeper who holds the puck with his hands for longer than three seconds shall be given a minor penalty.

(b) A goalkeeper must not deliberately hold the puck in any manner which in the opinion of the Referee causes a stoppage of play, nor throw the puck forward towards the opponents' goal, nor deliberately drop the puck into his pads or on to the goal net, nor deliberately pile up snow or obstacles at or near his net, that in the opinion of the Referee would tend to prevent the scoring of a goal.

(NOTE) *The object of this entire rule is to keep the puck in play continuously and any action taken by the goalkeeper which causes an unnecessary stoppage must be penalized without warning.*

(c) The penalty for infringement of this rule by the goalkeeper shall be a minor penalty.

(NOTE) *In the case of puck thrown forward by the goalkeeper being taken by an opponent, the Referee shall allow the resulting play to be completed, and if a goal is scored by the non-offending team, it shall be allowed and no penalty given; but if a goal is not scored, play shall be stopped and a minor penalty shall be imposed against the goalkeeper.*

(d) A minor penalty shall be imposed on a player except the goalkeeper who, while play is in progress, picks up the puck off the ice with his hand.

If a player, except the goal-keeper, while play is in progress, picks up the puck with his hand, from the ice in the goal crease area the play shall be stopped immediately and a penalty shot shall be awarded to the non-offending team.

(e) A player shall be permitted to stop or "bat" a puck in the air with his open hand, or push it along the ice with his hand, and the play shall not be stopped unless in the opinion of the Referee he has deliberately directed the puck to a teammate, in which case the play shall be stopped and the puck faced-off at the spot where the offense occurred.

(NOTE) *The object of this rule is to ensure continuous action and the Referee should NOT stop play unless he is satisfied that the directing of the puck to a teammate was in fact DELIBERATE.*

The puck may not be "batted" with the hand directly into the net at any time, but a goal shall be allowed when the puck has been legally "batted" or is deflected into the goal by a defending player except the goalkeeper.

Rule 58.   High Sticks

(a) The carrying of sticks above the normal height of the shoulder is prohibited, and a minor penalty may be imposed on any player violating this rule, at the discretion of the Referee.

(b) A goal scored from a stick so carried shall not be allowed, except by a player of the defending team.

(c) When a player carries or holds any part of his stick above the height of his shoulder so that injury to the face or head of an opposing player results, the Referee shall have no alternative but to impose a major penalty on the offending player. . . .

(d) Batting the puck above the normal height of the shoulders with the stick is prohibited and when it occurs there shall be a Whistle and ensuing face-off at the spot where the offense occurred unless:

1. the puck is batted to an opponent in which case the play shall continue.

2. a player of the defending side shall bat the puck into his own goal in which case the goal shall be allowed.

(NOTE) *When player bats the puck to an opponent under subsection 1 the Referee shall give the "wash-out" signal immediately. Otherwise he will stop the play.*

(e) When either team is below the numerical strength of its opponent and a player of the team of greater numerical strength causes a stoppage of play by striking the puck with his stick above the height of his shoulder, the resulting face-off shall be made at one of the end face-off spots adjacent to the goal of the team causing the stoppage.

Rule 59. Holding an Opponent

A minor penalty shall be imposed on a player who holds an opponent with hands or stick or in any other way.

Rule 60.   Hooking

(a) A minor penalty shall be imposed on any player who impedes or seeks to impede the progress of an opponent by "hooking" with his stick.

(b) A major penalty shall be imposed on any player who injures an opponent by "hooking." . . .

(NOTE) *When a player is checking another in such a way that there is only stick-to-stick contact such action is NOT either hooking or holding.*

Rule 61. Icing the Puck

(a) For the purpose of this rule, the center line will divide the ice into halves. Should any player of a team, equal or superior in numerical strength to the opposing team, shoot, bat, or deflect the puck from his own half of the ice, beyond the goal line of the opposing team, play shall be stopped and the puck faced off at the end face-off spot of the offending team, unless on the play the puck shall have entered the net of the opposing team, in which case the goal shall be allowed.

For the purpose of this rule the point of last contact with the puck by the team in possession shall be used to determine whether icing has occurred or not.

(NOTE 1) *If during the period of a delayed whistle due to a foul by a player of the side NOT in possession, the side in possession "ices" the puck then the face-off following the stoppage of play shall take place in the Neutral Zone near the Defending Blue Line of the team "icing" the puck.*

(NOTE 2) *When a team is "Short-handed" as the result of a penalty and the penalty is about to expire, the decision as to whether there has been an "icing" shall be determined at the instant the penalty expires, and if the puck crosses the opponent's goal line after the penalty has expired it is "icing." The action of the penalized player remaining in the penalty box will not alter the ruling.*

(NOTE 3) *For the purpose of interpretation of this rule "Icing the Puck" is completed the instant the puck is touched first by a defending player (other than the goalkeeper) after it has crossed the Goal Line and if in the action of so touching the puck it is knocked or deflected into the net it is NO goal.*

(NOTE 4) *When the puck is shot and rebounds from the body or sticks of an opponent in his own half of the ice so as to cross the goal line of the player shooting it shall not be considered as "icing."*

(NOTE 5) *Notwithstanding the provisions of this section concerning "batting" the puck in respect to the "icing the puck" rule, the provisions of the final paragraph of Rule 57 (e) apply and NO goal can be scored by batting the puck with the hand into the opponent's goal whether attended or not.*

(NOTE 6) *If while the Linesman has signaled a slow whistle for a clean interception under Rule 71 (c), the player intercepting shoots or bats the puck beyond the opponent's goal line in such a manner as to constitute "icing the puck," the Linesman's "slow whistle" shall be considered exhausted the instant the puck crosses the blue line and "icing" shall be called in the usual manner.*

(b) If a player of the side shooting the puck down the ice who is on-side and eligible to play the puck does so before it is touched by an opposing player, the play shall continue and it shall not be considered a violation of this rule.

(c) If the puck was so shot by a player of a side below the numerical strength of the opposing team, play shall continue and the face-off shall not take place.

(d) If, however, the puck shall go beyond the goal line in the opposite half of the ice directly from either of the players while facing off, it shall not be considered a violation of the rule.

(e) If, in the opinion of the Linesman, a player of the opposing team excepting the goalkeeper is able to play the puck before it passes his goal line, but has not done so, the face-off shall not be allowed and play shall continue. If, in the opinion of the Referee, the defending side intentionally abstains from playing the puck promptly when they are in a position to do so, he shall stop the play and order the resulting face-off on the adjacent corner face-off spot nearest the goal of the team at fault.

(NOTE) *The purpose of this section is to enforce continuous action and both Referee and Linesmen should interpret and apply the rule to produce this result.*

(f) If the puck shall touch any part of a player of the opposing side or his skates or his stick, or if it passes through any part of the goal crease before it shall have reached his goal line, or shall have touched the goalkeeper or his skates or his stick at any time before or after crossing his goal line it shall not be considered as "icing the puck" and play shall continue.

(NOTE) *If the goaltender takes any action to dislodge the puck from back of the nets the icing shall be washed out.*

(g) If the Linesman shall have erred in calling an "icing the puck" infraction (regardless of whether either team is short-handed) the puck shall be faced on the center ice face-off spot.

Rule 62.   Interference

(a) A minor penalty shall be imposed on a player who interferes with or impedes the progress of an opponent who is not in possession of the puck, or who deliberately knocks a stick out of an opponent's hand or who prevents a player who has dropped his stick from regaining possession of it or who knocks or shoots any abandoned or broken stick or illegal puck or other debris toward an opposing puck carrier in a manner that could cause him to be distracted. (see also Rule 80 (a).)

(NOTE) *The last player to touch the puck—other than a goalkeeper—shall be considered the player in possession. In interpreting this rule the Referee should make sure which of the players is the one creating the interference—often it is the action and movement of the attacking player which causes the interference since the defending players are entitled to "stand their ground" or "shadow" the attacking players. Players of the side in possession shall not be allowed to "run" deliberate interference for the puck carrier.*

(b) A minor penalty shall be imposed on any player on the players' bench or on the penalty bench who by means of his stick or his body interferes with the movements of the puck or of any opponent on the ice during the progress of play.

(c) A minor penalty shall be imposed on a player who, by means of his stick or his body, interferes with or impedes the movements of the goalkeeper by actual physical contact, while he is in his goal crease area unless the puck is already in that area.

(d) Unless the puck is in the goal crease area, a player of the attacking side not in possession may not stand on the goal crease line or in the goal crease or hold his stick in the goal crease area, and if the puck should enter the net while such condition prevails, a goal shall not be allowed, and the puck shall be faced-off in the neutral zone at the face-off spot nearest the attacking zone of the offending team.

(e) If a player of the attacking side has been physically interfered with by the action of any defending player so as to cause him to be in the goal crease, and the puck should enter the net while the player so interfered with is still within the goal crease, the "goal" shall be allowed.

(f) If when the goalkeeper has been removed from the ice any member of his team (including the goalkeeper) not legally on the ice, including the Manager, Coach or Trainer interferes by means of his body or stick or any other object with the movements of the puck or an opposing player, the Referee shall immediately award a goal to the non-offending team.

(g) When a player, in control of the puck in the opponent's side of the center red line, and having no other opponent to pass than the goalkeeper is interfered with by a stick or any part thereof or other object thrown or shot by any member of the defending team including the Manager, Coach, or Trainer, a penalty shot shall be awarded to the non-offending side.

(NOTE) *The attention of Referees is directed particularly to three types of offensive interference which should be penalized;*

(1) *When the defending team secures possession of the puck in its own end and the other players of that team run interference for the puck carrier by forming a protective screen against a forechecker;*

(2) *When a player facing off obstructs his opposite number*

after the face-off when the opponent is not in possession of the puck;

(3) *When the puck carrier makes a drop pass and follows through so as to make bodily contact with an opposing player.*

Defensive interference consists of bodily contact with an opposing player who is not in possession of the puck.

Rule 63. Interference by Spectators

(a) In the event of a player being held or interfered with by a spectator, the Referee or Linesman shall blow the whistle and play shall be stopped, unless the team of the player interfered with is in possession of the puck at this time when the play shall be allowed to be completed before blowing the whistle, and the puck shall be faced at the spot where last played at time of stoppage.

(NOTE) *The Referee shall report to the President for disciplinary action all cases in which a player becomes involved in an altercation with a spectator but no penalty should be imposed.*

(b) In the event that objects are thrown on the ice which interfere with the progress of the game the Referee shall blow the whistle and stop the play, and the puck shall be faced-off at the spot play is stopped.

Rule 64. Kicking Player

A match penalty shall be imposed on any player who kicks or attempts to kick another player.

(NOTE) *Whether or not an injury occurs the Referee may, at his discretion, impose a ten minute time penalty under this rule.*

Rule 65.   Kicking Puck

Kicking the puck shall be permitted in all zones, but a goal may not be scored by the kick of an attacking player except if an attacking player kicks the puck and it is deflected into the net by any players of the defending side except the goalkeeper.

Rule 66. Leaving Players' Bench or Penalty Bench

(a) No player may leave the players' bench or penalty bench at any time during an altercation. Substitutions made prior to the altercation shall be permitted provided the players so substituting do not enter the altercation.

(b) For violation of this rule a Double Minor penalty shall be imposed on the player of the team who was first to leave the players' bench or penalty bench during an altercation. If players of both teams leave their respective benches at the same time, the first identifiable player of each team to do so shall incur a Double Minor penalty. A Game Misconduct penalty shall also be imposed on any player who is penalized under this subsection.

(c) Any player (other than those dealt with under subsection (b) hereof) who leaves his players' bench during an altercation and is assessed a minor, major or misconduct penalty for his actions, shall also incur an automatic Game Misconduct penalty.

(d) [Regarding] a player (other than those dealt with under subsection (b) & (c) hereof) who leaves his players' bench during an altercation . . . the Referee shall report all such infractions to the President who shall have full power to impose such further penalty as he shall deem appropriate.

(NOTE 1) *This [is] in addition to the normal penalties imposed for fouls committed by the player after he has left the players' bench.*

(NOTE 2) *For the purpose of determining which player was first to leave his players' bench during an altercation the Referee may consult with the Linesmen or Minor Officials.*

(e) In regular League games, any player who incurs a *second* penalty under subsection (b) hereof (for leaving the players' bench first) shall be suspended automatically for the next League game of his team. For each subsequent violation, the automatic suspension shall be increased by one game.

In play-off games, any player who incurs a penalty under subsection (b) hereof (for leaving the players' bench first), shall be suspended automatically for the next play-off game of his team. For each subsequent violation, this automatic suspension shall be increased by one game.

The automatic suspensions incurred under this subsection in respect to League games shall have no effect with respect to violations during play-off games.

(f) Except at the end of each period, or on expiration of penalty, no player may at any time leave the penalty bench.

(g) A penalized player who leaves the penalty bench before his penalty has expired, whether play is in progress or not, shall incur an additional minor penalty, after serving his unexpired penalty.

(h) Any penalized player leaving the penalty bench during stoppage of play and during an altercation shall incur a minor penalty plus a Game Misconduct penalty after serving his unexpired time.

(i) If a player leaves the penalty bench before his penalty is fully served, the Penalty Timekeeper shall note the time and signal the Referee who will immediately stop play.

(j) In the case of player returning to the ice before his time has expired through an error of the Penalty Timekeeper, he is not to serve an additional penalty, but must serve his unexpired time.

(k) If a player of an attacking side in possession of the puck shall be in such a position as to have no opposition between him and the opposing goalkeeper, and while in such position he shall be interfered with by a player of the opposing side who shall have illegally entered the game, the Referee shall impose a penalty shot against the side to which the offending player belongs.

(l) If the opposing goalkeeper has been removed and an attacking player in possession of the puck shall have no player of the defending team to pass and a stick or a part thereof or any other object is thrown or shot by an opposing player or the player is fouled from behind thereby being prevented from having a clear shot on an open goal, a goal shall be awarded against the offending team.

If when the opposing goalkeeper has been removed from the ice a player of the side attacking the unattended goal is interfered with by a player who shall have entered the game illegally, the Referee shall immediately award a goal to the non-offending team.

(m) If a Coach or Manager gets on the ice after the start of a period and before that period is ended the Referee shall impose a bench minor penalty against the team

and report the incident to the President for disciplinary action. . . .

(o) If a penalized player returns to the ice from the penalty bench before his penalty has expired by his own error or the error of the Penalty Timekeeper, any goal scored by his own team while he is illegally on the ice shall be disallowed but all penalties imposed on either team shall be served as regular penalties.

(p) If a player shall illegally enter the game from his own players' bench or from the penalty bench, any goal scored by his own team while he is illegally on the ice shall be disallowed, but all penalties imposed on either team shall be served as regular penalties.

Rule 67. Molesting Officials

(a) Any player who touches or holds a Referee, Linesman or any game official with his hand or his stick or trips or body-checks any of such officials, shall receive a ten-minute Misconduct Penalty or a Game Misconduct Penalty. The use of a substitute for the player so suspended shall be permitted.

(b) Any Club Executive, Manager, Coach or Trainer who holds or strikes an official shall be automatically suspended from the game, [and] ordered to the dressing room . . .

Rule 68. Obscene or Profane Language or Gestures

(a) Players shall not use obscene gestures on the ice or anywhere in the rink before, during or after the game. For a violation of this rule a game misconduct penalty shall be imposed and the Referee shall report the circumstances to the President of the League for further disciplinary action.

(b) Players shall not use profane language on the ice or anywhere in the rink before, during or after a game. For violation of this Rule, a Misconduct Penalty shall be imposed except when the violation occurs in the vicinity of the players' bench in which case a bench minor penalty shall be imposed.

(NOTE) *It is the responsibility of all game officials and all Club officials to send a confidential report to the President setting out the full details concerning the use of obscene gestures or language by any player, Coach or other official. The President shall take such further disciplinary action as he shall deem appropriate.*

(c) Club Executives, Managers, Coaches and Trainers shall not use obscene or profane language or gestures anywhere in the rink. For violation of this rule a bench minor penalty shall be imposed.

Rule 69.   Off-Sides

(a) The position of the player's skates and not that of his stick shall be the determining factor in all instances in deciding an "off-side." A player is off-side when both skates are completely over the outer edge of the determining center line or blue line involved in the play.

(NOTE 1) *A player is "on-side" when "either" of his skates are in contact with or on his own side of the line at the instant the puck completely crosses the outer edge of that line regardless of the position of his stick.*

(NOTE 2) *It should be noted that while the position of the player's skates is what determines whether a player is "off-side,"* *nevertheless the question of "off-side" never arises until the puck has completely crossed the outer edge of the line at which time the decision is to be made.*

(b) If in the opinion of the Linesman an intentional off-side play has been made, the puck shall be faced-off at the end face-off spot in the defending zone of the offending team.

(NOTE 3) *This rule does not apply to a team below the numerical strength of its opponent. In such cases the puck shall be faced-off at the spot from which the pass was made.*

(NOTE 4) *An intentional off-side is one which is made for the purpose of securing a stoppage of play regardless of the reason, or where an off-side play is made under conditions where there is no possibility of completing a legal pass.*

(c) If the linesmen shall have erred in calling an off-side pass infraction (regardless of whether either team is short-handed) the puck shall be faced on the center ice face-off spot.

Rule 70.   Passes

(a) The puck may be passed by any player to a player of the same side within any one of the three zones into which the ice is divided, but may not be passed forward from a player in one zone to a player of the same side in another zone, except by a player on the defending team, who may make and take forward passes from his own defending zone to the center line without incurring an off-side penalty. This "forward pass" from the Defending Zone must be completed by the pass receiver who is legally on-side at the center line.

(NOTE 1) *The position of the puck (not the player's skates) shall be the determining factor in deciding from which zone the pass was made.*

(NOTE 2) *Passes may be completed legally at the center red line in exactly the same manner as passes at the attacking blue line.*

(b) Should the puck, having been passed, contact any part of the body, stick or skates of a player of the same side who is legally on-side, the pass shall be considered to have been completed.

(c) The player last touched by the puck shall be deemed to be in possession.

Rebounds off a goalkeeper's pads or other equipment shall not be considered as a change of possession or the completion of the play by the team when applying Rule 34 (b).

(d) If a player in the Neutral Zone is preceded into the Attacking Zone by the puck passed from the Neutral Zone he shall be eligible to take possession of the puck anywhere in the Attacking Zone except when the "Icing the Puck" rule applies.

(e) If a player in the same zone from which a pass is made is preceded by the puck into succeeding zones he shall be eligible to take possession of the puck in that zone except where the "Icing the Puck" rule applies.

(f) If an attacking player passes the puck backward toward his own goal from the Attacking Zone, an opponent may play the puck anywhere regardless of whether he (the opponent) was in the same zone at the time the puck was passed or not. (*No "slow whistle"*).

Rule 71. Preceding Puck into Attacking Zone

(a) Players of an attacking team must not precede the puck into the Attacking Zone.

(b) For violation of this rule, the play is stopped, and puck shall be faced-off in the Neutral Zone at the face-off spot nearest the Attacking Zone of the offending team.

(NOTE) *A player actually propelling the puck who shall cross the line ahead of the puck, shall not be considered "off-side."*

(c) If, however, notwithstanding the fact that a member of the attacking team shall have preceded the puck into the Attacking Zone, the puck be cleanly intercepted by a member of the defending team at or near the blue line, and be carried or passed by him into the Neutral Zone the "off-side" shall be ignored and play permitted to continue.

(*Officials will carry out this rule by means of the "slow whistle"*).

(d) If a player legally carries or passes the puck back into his own Defending Zone while a player of the opposing team is in such Defending Zone, the "off-side" shall be ignored and play permitted to continue.

(*No "slow whistle"*).

Rule 72. Puck Out of Bounds or Unplayable

(a) When the puck goes outside the playing area at either end or either side of the rink or strikes any obstacles above the playing surface other than the boards, glass or wire, it shall be faced-off from whence it was shot or deflected, unless otherwise expressly provided in these rules.

(b) When the puck becomes lodged in

the netting on the outside of either goal so as to make it unplayable, or if it is frozen between opposing players intentionally or otherwise, the Referee shall stop the play and face-off the puck at either of the adjacent face-off spots unless in the opinion of the Referee the stoppage was caused by a player of the attacking team, in which case the resulting face-off shall be conducted in the Neutral Zone.

(NOTE) *This includes stoppage of play caused by a player of the attacking side shooting the puck on to the back of the defending team's net without any intervening action by the defending team.*

The defending team and/or the attacking team may play the puck off the net at any time. However, should the puck remain on the net for longer than three seconds, play shall be stopped and the face-off shall take place in the end face-off zone except when the stoppage is caused by the attacking team, then the face-off shall take place on a face-off spot in the neutral zone.

(c) A minor penalty shall be imposed on a goalkeeper who deliberately drops the puck on the goal netting to cause a stoppage of play.

(d) If the puck comes to rest on top of the boards surrounding the playing area it shall be considered to be in play and may be played legally by hand or stick.

Rule 73.   Puck Must Be Kept in Motion

(a) The puck must at all times be kept in motion.

(b) Except to carry the puck behind its goal once, a side in possession of the puck in its own defense area shall always advance the puck towards the opposing goal, except if it shall be prevented from so doing by players of the opposing side.

For the first infraction of this rule play shall be stopped and a face-off shall be made at either end face-off spot adjacent to the goal of the team causing the stoppage, and the Referee shall warn the Captain or Alternate Captain of the offending team of the reason for the face-off. For a second violation by any player of the same team in the same period a minor penalty shall be imposed on the player violating the rule.

(c) A minor penalty shall be imposed on any player including the goalkeeper who holds, freezes or plays the puck with his stick, skates or body along the boards in such a manner as to cause a stoppage of play unless he is actually being checked by an opponent.

(d) A player beyond his defense area shall not pass nor carry the puck backward into his Defense Zone for the purpose of delaying the game except when his team is below the numerical strength of the opponents on the ice.

(e) For an infringement of this rule, the face-off shall be at the nearest end face-off spot in the Defending Zone of the offending team.

Rule 74.   Puck Out of Sight and Illegal Puck

(a) Should a scramble take place, or a player accidentally fall on the puck, and the puck be out of sight of the Referee, he shall immediately blow his whistle and stop the play. The puck shall then be "faced-off" at the point where the play was stopped, unless otherwise provided for in the rules.

(b) If at any time while play is in progress a puck other than the one legally in play shall appear on the playing surface, the play shall not be stopped but shall continue with the legal puck until the play then in progress is completed by change of possession.

Rule 75. Puck Striking Official

Play shall not be stopped if the puck touches an official anywhere on the rink, regardless of whether a team is short-handed or not.

Rule 76. Refusing to Start Play

(a) If, when both teams are on the ice, one team for any reason shall refuse to play when ordered to do so by the Referee, he shall warn the Captain or Alternate Captain and allow the team so refusing fifteen seconds within which to begin the game or resume play. If at the end of that time the team shall still refuse to play, the Referee shall impose a two-minute penalty on a player of the offending team to be designated by the Manager or Coach of that team, through the playing Captain; and should there be a [fourth] repetition of the same incident the Referee shall . . . have no alternative but to declare that the game be forfeited to the non-offending club, and the case shall be reported to the President for further action.

(b) If a team, when ordered to do so by the Referee, through its Club Executive, Manager or Coach, fails to go on the ice, and start play within five minutes . . . the game shall be forfeited, and the case shall be reported to the President for further action.

(NOTE) *The President of the League shall issue instructions pertaining to records, etc., of a forfeited game.*

Rule 77. Slashing

(a) A minor or major penalty, at the discretion of the Referee, shall be imposed on any player who impedes or seeks to impede the progress of an opponent by "slashing" with his stick.

(b) A major penalty shall be imposed on any player who injures an opponent by slashing. . . .

(NOTE) *Referees should penalize as "slashing" any player who swings his stick at any opposing player (whether in or out of range) without actually striking him or where a player on the pretext of playing the puck makes a wild swing at the puck with the object of intimidating an opponent.*

(c) Any player who swings his stick at another player in the course of any altercation shall be subject [to] suspension, to be imposed by the President.

(NOTE) *The Referee shall impose the normal appropriate penalty provided in the other sections of this rule and shall in addition report promptly to the President all infractions under this section.*

Rule 78. Spearing

(a) A major penalty shall be imposed on a player who spears or attempts to spear an opponent.

(NOTE) *"Attempt to spear" shall include all cases where a spearing gesture is made regardless whether bodily contact is made or not. . . .*

(NOTE) *"Spearing" shall mean stabbing an opponent with the point of the stick blade while the stick is being carried with one hand or both hands.*

(NOTE) *Spearing may also be treated as a "deliberate attempt to injure" under Rule 44.*

Rule 79.   Start of Game and Periods

(a) The game shall be commenced at the time scheduled by a "face-off" in the center of the rink and shall be renewed promptly at the conclusion of each intermission in the. same manner.

No delay shall be permitted by reason of any ceremony, exhibition, demonstration or presentation unless consented to reasonably in advance by the visiting team.

(b) Home clubs shall have the choice of goals to defend at the start of the game except where both players' benches are on the same side of the rink, in which case the home club shall start the game defending the goal nearest to its own bench. The teams shall change ends for each succeeding regular or overtime period.

(c) During the pre-game warm-up (which shall not exceed twenty minutes in duration) and before the commencement of play in any period each team shall confine its activity to its own end of the rink so as to ieave clear an area thirty feet wide across the center of the Neutral Zone.

(NOTE 1) *The Game Timekeeper shall be responsible for signaling the commencement and termination of the pre-game warm-up and any violation of this rule by the players shall be reported to the President by the Supervisor when in attendance at the game.*

(NOTE 2) *Players shall not be permitted to come on the ice during a stoppage in play or at the end of the first and second periods for the purpose of warming-up. The Referee will report any violation of this rule to the President for disciplinary action.*

(d) Fifteen minutes before the time scheduled for the start of the game both teams shall vacate the ice and proceed to their dressing rooms while the ice is being flooded. Both teams shall be signaled by the Game Timekeeper to return to the ice together in time for the scheduled start of the game. . . .

Rule 80.   Throwing Stick

(a) When any player of the defending side, including the goalkeeper or Manager, Coach or Trainer, deliberately throws or shoots his stick or any part thereof or any other object at the puck in his Defending Zone, the Referee shall allow the play to be completed and if a goal is not scored a penalty shot shall be awarded to the non-offending side, which shot shall be taken by the player designated by the Referee as the player fouled.

If, however, the goal being unattended and the attacking player having no defending player to pass and having a chance to score on an "open net," a stick or part thereof or any other object be thrown by a defending player thereby preventing a shot on the "open net" a goal shall be awarded to the attacking side.

(NOTE 1) *If the officials are unable to determine the person against whom the offense was made the offended team through the Captain shall designate the player on the ice at the time the offense was committed who will take the shot.*

(NOTE 2) *For the purpose of this rule, an open net is defined as one from which a goaltender has been removed for an additional attacking player.*

(b) A major penalty shall be imposed on any player *on the ice* who throws his stick or any part thereof or any other object in the direction of the puck carrier in any zone, except when such act has been penalized by the assessment of a penalty shot or the award of a goal.

(NOTE) *When a player discards the broken portion of a stick by tossing it to the side of the ice (and not over the boards) in such a way as will not interfere with play or opposing player, no penalty will be imposed for so doing.*

(c) The Referee and Linesmen shall report promptly to the President for disciplinary action every case where a stick or any part thereof is thrown outside the playing area.

Rule 81. Time of Match

(a) The time allowed for a game shall be three twenty-minute periods of actual play with a rest intermission between periods.

Play shall be resumed promptly following each intermission upon the expiry of fifteen minutes from the completion of play in the preceding period. A preliminary warning shall be given by the Game Timekeeper to the officials and to both teams three minutes prior to the resumption of play in each period and the final warning shall be given in sufficient time to enable the teams to resume play promptly. . . .

(b) The team scoring the greatest number of goals during the three twenty-minute periods shall be the winner, and shall be credited with two points in the League standing.

(c) In the intervals between periods, the ice surface shall be flooded unless mutually agreed to the contrary.

(d) If any unusual delay occurs within five minutes of the end of the first or second periods the Referee may order the next regular intermission to be taken immediately and the balance of the period will be completed on the resumption of play with the teams defending the same goals, after which the teams will change ends and resume play of the ensuing period without delay.

(NOTE) *If a delay takes place with more than five minutes remaining in the first or second period, the Referee will order the next regular intermission to be taken immediately only when requested to do so by the Home Club.*

Rule 82. Tied Games

(a) If, at the end of the three regular twenty-minute periods, the score shall be tied, the game shall be called a "TIE," and each team shall be credited with one point in the League standing.

(b) Special conditions for duration and number of periods of play-off games, shall be arranged by the Board of Governors.

Rule 83. Tripping

(a) A minor penalty shall be imposed on any player who shall place his stick, knee, foot, arm, hand or elbow in such a manner that it shall cause his opponent to trip or fall.

(NOTE) *If in the opinion of the Referee a player is unquestionably hook-checking the puck and obtains possession of it, thereby tripping the puck carrier, no penalty shall be imposed.*

(b) When a player, in control of the puck in the opponent's side of the center red line, and having no other opponent to pass than the goalkeeper, is tripped or otherwise fouled from behind thus preventing a reasonable scoring opportunity a penalty shot shall be awarded to the non-offending side. Nevertheless the Referee shall not stop the play until the attacking side has lost possession of the puck to the defending side.

(NOTE 1) *The intention of this rule is to restore a reasonable scoring opportunity which has been lost by reason of a foul from behind when the foul is committed in the opponent's side of the center red line.*

*By "control of the puck" is meant the act of propelling the puck with the stick. If while it is being propelled the puck is touched by another player or his equipment or hits the goal or goes free the player shall no longer be consid-*ered to be "in control of the puck."

(NOTE 2) *Accidental trips occurring simultaneously with or after stoppage of play will not be penalized.*

(c) If, when the opposing goalkeeper has been removed from the ice, a player in control of the puck is tripped or otherwise fouled with no opposition between him and the opposing goal, thus preventing a reasonable scoring opportunity, the Referee shall immediately stop the play and award a goal to the attacking team.

Rule 84.   Unnecessary Roughness

At the discretion of the Referee, a minor penalty may be imposed on any player deemed guilty of unnecessary roughness.